The Power of Business Rapport

Also by Dr. Michael Brooks

INSTANT RAPPORT

THE POWER OF
BUSINESS
RAPPORT

Use NLP Technology to
Make More Money, Sell Yourself
and Your Product,
and Move Ahead in Business

DR. MICHAEL BROOKS

HarperCollins*Publishers*

FIRST EDITION

Designed by C. Linda Dingler

LIBRARY OF CONGRESS CATALOGING-IN-PUBLICATION DATA
Brooks, Michael.
  The power of business rapport / Michael Brooks.—1st ed.
    p. cm.
  Includes index.
  ISBN 0–06–016383–6
  1. Business communications—Psychological aspects.
2. Interpersonal relations. 3. Nonverbal communication.
4. Neurolinguistic programming. I. Title.
HF5718.B735 1991
650.1′3—dc20   90–55528

---

91 92 93 94 95 CC/HC 10 9 8 7 6 5 4 3 2 1

This book is dedicated to

SHOSHONE LONGFELLOW BROOKS, g.r.*
whose love, companionship, and loyalty
blesses my life.

and to

BUMMY
—wherever I may find her.

*golden retriever

Contents

Acknowledgments

I am very pleased to have been given the opportunity to write another book on NeuroLinguistic Programming. My belief and dedication to it are simply the result of having used it so successfully in so many areas of my life.

I think that when one discovers something very significant, and moreover something that causes good to come from it, one automatically desires to share the wealth with as many as possible. This book is nothing more than the result of wanting others to benefit from its beautiful collective technology.

Thanks are due the following:

My literary agent, Al Lowman.

My editor, Cynthia Barrett, who, besides contributing her editorial expertise, made it safe and pleasurable for me to write this book.

Lara Amber Ewing, NLP trainer par excellence.

Connirae and Steve Andreas of Colorado.

My gratitude and heartfelt thanks to Andy Bherman, who, by virtue of his superior wizardry, literally opened the space for this work to have the forum that it has enjoyed.

I am grateful and want to acknowledge Dr. John Grinder and Richard Bandler for conceiving the model of NLP.

Thanks to B. G. Dilworth of Authors and Artists Group for his good care. And my appreciation to Barbara Waggoner for kindling the fire of curiosity that led to my further discoveries in NLP.

To Graham Kavanagh for getting me clear that all the insights in the world were meaningless unless acted upon.

I would like to express my gratitude to HarperCollins, for publishing my work.

My family and friends all contributed to this work in one way or another. Certainly they gave of their time and patience, and often pointed me in the right direction. When I needed the rhyme of grim intention, my mother reminded me of who I am, and what I had to offer. Thanks, mom.

And finally to everyone who was there from the beginning; and to all who chose to wish me well and support me and nurture me, thank you all so much and God bless you.

Preface

In the early seventies—nobody really knows the exact date—
in northern California, two academicians developed a behavioral science that had no name, but was acknowledged by
many to be very powerful. Inherent in this breakthrough
psychology was its ability to utilize ordinary everyday language and nonverbal behavior to gain tremendous leverage
and power over those personal and business relationships to
which it was applied.

Years went by, and the two scientists—a computer math-
ematician and a linguistics scholar—gained local reputation
as being the fathers of a brilliant new form of humanistic
psychology. And indeed they had given life to something
wonderful. The academic community, as well as many fascinated parties in the professional and private sectors, em-
braced the model as creative and inventive, but most of all
as awesome. Because of the potential of this process, and the
possibility of its misuse, people intimate with it, as well as its
creators, felt the need to cloak it in a shroud of mystery, and
this first generation of practitioners were successful at keeping it largely unknown—to be doled out as they saw fit.

Some few years later, the process—now known as
NeuroLinguistic Programming, or NLP—broke through the
silence in spite of itself, and people in the psychological and
psychiatric community began learning and adapting it to fit
various needs. It was called NLP (neuro = behavior, linguistic = language, programming = altering change) because it
gave access to others' perceptual codes, so that we could

reprogram their behavior through our language and actions. At this point in time, NLP's creators, Dr. John Grinder and Richard Bandler, had ceded some of their knowledge to a "second generation" of psychological practitioners, who further expanded many of NLP's applications. A flurry of books appeared at this time, mostly published by small and obscure book houses, with titles and text that further mystified NLP's use.

During this period, Bandler and Grinder took NLP on the road, doing some evening, weekend, and week-long presentations in California. A lot of money was being made on NLP then, yet few people who attempted to learn it succeeded in truly mastering its power.

This was interesting for several reasons.

There was now a developing body of work on the subject, albeit somewhat vague in content, and many people were reading and studying NLP in addition to taking training in it. In fact, these "courses" had three levels: practitioner, master practitioner, and trainer. To reach the top of the tree, one had to commit some three years of study and roughly $15,000—if one could locate a place that offered this sort of education. Which brings up another interesting fact: There was no authority empowered to grant an institution the "right" to teach and confer a degree in NLP. This led to various schools popping up across the country, oftentimes run out of makeshift office space, that advertised themselves as NLP training centers. Some even received the blessing of either Bandler or Grinder, who by now had parted ways and theory and, for all intents and purposes, remained out of reach of the common devotee. But most of the NLP centers were, and are, run by those who simply consider themselves to be qualified teaching professionals.

In the years that followed, NLP became more widely known through the efforts of people who, in my opinion, truly wanted others to benefit from it. Most notably, these include the Andreases of Colorado; the brilliant work of Robert Dilts; and Leslie Cameron-Bandler's worthwhile contributions.

It is true that NLP can be misused. It is by its very nature a covert art, and hence there will be those who will learn it and then abuse the privilege of its power. Such is the nature of our species. But let me say that I've observed NLP being used in *service* to society ten times more than I've witnessed it being used to its detriment.

When you learn the mysteries I've unraveled for you in this book, I think you'll find that NeuroLinguistic Programming will be something that adds immeasurably to the quality of your life. In its business applications, there is nothing that even comes close to NLP's power, efficacy, and ease of use. Moreover, you are limited only by your imagination in adapting and expanding on its technologies for your own personal use, for NLP, once learned, evolves with you as you evolve.

When I first discovered NLP, I was overjoyed. I knew that here was a great tool that could benefit society as well as individuals. I also knew that with its acquisition came great responsibility. I'd like to pass that on to you: Learn this technology well, making full use of what I offer you, and experience the personal power that NLP will give you—but temper it also with restraint. If you adhere to this credo, your business and your life, if the two can be separated, will immeasurably prosper.

MICHAEL JONATHAN BROOKS
BRIDGEHAMPTON, NEW YORK, 1991

1

INTRODUCTION

You know that man or woman at the office who's really making it? The one who constantly gets ahead—despite the fact you can't find one redeeming quality about him? You know who I mean. For some reason, no matter what he does, he's always getting the nod from the boss. When a really terrific opportunity comes along, you can bet he's the one who gets first crack at it. And even though he fails sometimes, he's always considered for the next top project. It makes you wonder what he's got going for him. He's not particularly brilliant. Didn't come out of Wharton. Seniority? Not really. Then what's the deal here? What's he got that you don't, anyway?

Well, if you take a close look you might discover that he is where he is because he's got something you don't have—at the moment. He's in *rapport* with those who make a difference in his life. He's able to consistently sell himself not only to the boss, but to his colleagues and clients as well, because he knows what it takes and what to do to get these people to agree with him. Or at least see things from his point of view. He's able to *enroll* them in his plan of action because he's skilled at ascertaining what it takes to jump onto the same wavelength of the person he's relating to. And once he's in rapport, all he does is the mechanical nuts and bolts part of the job, just like the rest of us do. The net result is that he doesn't do anything really differently than us. But because of his skills in creating *rapport,* he always gets the *opportunity.*

That's what this book is about: how to create immense power in business through rapport and maximize the opportunity it provides.

Opportunity is always there. Sometimes it's hidden in the conference room or in the board of directors meetings. It's practically always present when you interact with a potential customer or client. And it's something that you have at your fingertips when you're one on one with your boss. Opportunity is not an event waiting to happen—it already exists as a part of human dynamics. But using the gift of opportunity is another thing entirely. This is where most of us fail. We don't know how to maximize an unfolding opportunity because we never really learned how to recognize it. Think about that. When were you taught to see opportunity, let alone use it? Don't despair. You're about to learn a skill that will change the way you think about opportunity. And when you use this skill, the door of opportunity will blow wide open for you.

The Power of Business Rapport is about the powerful application of NeuroLinguistic Programming, or NLP, to business. It is the first book of its kind to adapt the theories and applications from this science into a practical and highly effective methodology.

NLP will give you the power to change people's experience of you so that customer, colleague, and executive resistance will disappear. Moreover, it will allow you to influence and persuade people in a way that you probably had never thought possible. In turn, this will allow you to produce the following results:

- Higher income, because you'll be able to put ideas into action that are more creative and profitable *for you* rather than yielding to what others consider worthwhile.

- More often than not, you'll be playing the game by *your* rules rather than being an unwitting participant in the games others want to play.

- You'll communicate more effectively, thereby engaging people in an understated and unconscious, yet highly getable manner.

- A measurable reduction in anxiety associated with business endeavors. Armed with this technology, you'll feel self-assured in a way that produces calm and certainty.

Nowhere in life, except possibly in personal relationships, is the notion of rapport more germane than in the *business* of life. Successful chairmen and executives, managers and presidents, have long known this. However, they practice it intuitively or involuntarily. Only a scarce few understand what it is—and still fewer, how to create it.

In many ways, business demands an even more exacting and facile use of rapport skills than do our personal lives. Indeed, an argument could be made that without business rapport, the other parts of our lives would suffer as a result of our not being able to produce.

Rapport in the business realm is more important today than ever. The old "jack 'em up and glaze 'em over" techniques of salesmanship just don't cut it now. High-pressure tactics and quick closings have gone the way of the vacuum tube. Buyers want more of a *sense* of things; they want a "high-touch" parameter as part of the sale, much like value-added merchandising. You could say that adding value through rapport is really what selling is about today: a process whereby goods and services are bought and sold through trust, confidence, and understanding. Without rapport, these conditions simply cannot be realized.

In my first book, *Instant Rapport*, I built a model of behavior whereby results are achieved in one's personal life by weaving the dynamics of NLP into the fabric of personal relationships. One of the most obvious—even imperative—realizations of that book was how significant it would be to have this technology available to us within the context of business. It is the purpose of *The Power of Business Rapport* to fulfill that objective.

This book offers an applied technology that gives you the actual know-how to take control of your business affairs and charge them with the power to make more money, move ahead, get promoted, and generally reclaim the esteem you may have lost with failed business opportunities. It's about creating money and opportunity through rapport, and it will transform the way you do business as an individual and as an organization, forever. That is the main thrust of our work here: mobilizing the newly harnessed power of rapport to get results. Because today, more than ever before, in business—as in life itself—where there is no rapport, there is no sale.

NLP is a technology that allows us to influence, persuade, reposition, and finalize any deal with a quarter of the effort, in half the time, with better understanding, and with more positive results than you've ever thought feasible. This is possible because NLP's power appeals to people on *their* map of reality. When two parties to any transaction are in rapport—that is, when they are operating on the same wavelength—the probability of successfully completing that transaction is enormously magnified. NLP, a model of behavior that allows us to achieve immediate connection and thus influence others, is the invisible catalyst that brings people together by maximizing commonality and minimizing disparity. NLP is a cutting edge process that takes previously irreparable conflicts and transforms them into solvable communication—producing positive results. It is, according to most experts in the field, the most innovative and advanced, easy-to-learn and powerful business tool available for the production of rapport, and hence the stuff of which successful careers are made.

The following are just a few examples of business situations where people can truly benefit from the skills taught in this book.

- The salesman who will increase his sales through the use of strategy elicitation, then influence his boss to promote him by anchoring an embedded suggestion.

- The secretary who sells her boss on the idea that she can do more than just type. She'll use NLP to enhance her persuasiveness and run her boss's promotion strategy.

- The vice president who will finally convince the finance committee about his ideas for the fall campaign. He'll mirror the committee members through an impressive display of pacing and leading. Then he'll use power language to design an ad campaign that reaches people on all three representational levels.

- The trial lawyer who'll win more and more cases because her rapport skills with the judge and jury are super-effective. She'll use the full array of NLP technologies in cross-examination and in her closing argument.

- The customer relations manager whose department will consistently outperform itself with the use of anchoring to fire off consumer satisfaction strategies.

- The educator who will effectively reach her students and make learning fun as she unpacks their learning strategies and plays them back while teaching.

- And, ultimately, our business selves, though it doesn't matter what we sell. Underneath our presentation, what we ultimately offer for sale is who we are. Using NLP, you'll be able to sell at the level of self and watch your results skyrocket.

Now let me tell you about my personal discovery of NeuroLinguistic Programming.

Before going into business, I was a clinical psychologist, devoting most of my time to private clients. I found satisfaction in my work, and it gave me the opportunity to experience many different fields of endeavor. While being a psychologist was, in its own very special way, rewarding, I grew restless with it. I wanted to expand my horizons, and I found it terribly frustrating to be so limited. However, I pushed on, and did indeed—shortly before leaving my practice—move into other areas of exploration. This is probably when the whole concept of interpersonal psychology first began to enchant me.

But straight around the corner was the business world. And what a world. It was unlike anything else I had ever been drawn to. I saw it as the realm of the impossibly possible. Anything could be accomplished. It was in sharp contrast to my rather linear psychological practice, and I was fascinated by the results I could produce. Suddenly I was involved in a myriad of entrepreneurial transactions, first as a consultant, then as a player. Much of my success could be attributed to the fact that I was using my knowledge of people dynamics to get amazing things done. Things that took other people years to learn and months to accomplish took me days to execute. The whole notion of long decision-making periods completely disappeared. Motivating people became second nature and quite natural. And implementing new concepts became easy. I was producing positive working results at an accelerated and amazing speed. I was intoxicated.

One fall I visited some friends in Vermont. I couldn't have known it then, but this was the beginning of a new journey.

During the weekend, while waiting to meet a friend for lunch near the hamlet of Hawk Mountain, I found myself with a few hours to kill and wandered into what, for all intents and purposes, was an obscure and reverent psychological library. I don't know why, but I thought it curious to so casually have chanced upon such a marvelous place; indeed, I felt enchantingly at home. The place, like many establishments in Vermont, felt warm and inviting, and I browsed among the many stacks of the new and old.

While searching for a journal or quarterly that might bring me up to date on what was new in my area of interest, cognitive styles, I chanced upon an article that went on at some length about how we represent experience to ourselves, and how that related to the way we see the world. It grabbed my attention, for it was concisely novel and talked about the neurology of relationship. I must have read way past my time, for the outside light shifted, and I knew I had to be on my way. But when I left that place, with its warm and protective atmosphere, I knew I was taking something with me— something that I had been searching for, something that would have a profound and transforming effect on my life. This was my first encounter with NLP.

I set about the task of learning as much as I could about this amazing new field, eagerly inquiring where I could find out more about it. And that was to be my first barrier. No one—not a soul—knew anything about it. Not universities, not analytic institutes, not colleagues or friends. Most people either thought I wanted information about computers or brain surgery or a foreign language. I found this bizarre. But I was persistent. I knew I had unwittingly tapped into something that was going to be unbelievably valuable. The question was: What to do next?

I continued to struggle through journals, through cross-references, through largely unknown and rare monographs. I gradually pieced together a semblance of a frame within which to work. And work is precisely what it turned out to be. At the beginning, just finding bits and pieces of clues was the most I was able to accomplish. But gradually the puzzle began taking on some form. Still, it was slow going. Following up on the various authors' references proved to be a monumental task. And oftentimes, when I was successful at discovering its whereabouts, a source would prove to be erroneous. Then one day a good friend, who knew about my research, gave me a book he found at a store downtown, and this proved to be my first big breakthrough. Reading it, though, was an experience in and of itself. Because it was attempting to discuss a *process,* initially I found the book quite difficult to fully understand. Finally, after some time and many rereadings, I got a handle on what it was about. It also directed me to further sources of information on NLP. Months went by in which I found a source here, a paper there. All the while, one thought grew larger and larger in my mind: Why wasn't this wonderful knowledge more widely known, and why was it couched in such secrecy?

At the same time, there were some very interesting events taking place in my life. In fact, they were so subtle that perhaps they had been there for some time but existed in some peripheral part of my consciousness; certainly they were out of the conscious portion of my attention.

My level of *rapport* with others was incredible. I was connecting to people, able to really be on the same wavelength with them. My presentation became clear and concise, because my thoughts were well articulated. I had undergone a transformation that would forever alter the outcome of my self.

And this produced two distinct results.

First, my personal relationships completely changed. Right across the board. I was able to bring anyone I chose into a total and high rapport simply by engaging the principles I acquired by reformulating NLP. My old friends wanted to strengthen our bonds; new ones wanted to create firmer foundations. My relationships with women became a place that was very comfortable and satisfying—not only for me, but for the women with whom I related. Out of all this grew an unusually effective man, someone who plays the game at cause, not at effect.

Second, I again grew very successful in business. And this too was totally a function of the use of NLP. While it was true that I began again to involve myself in entrepreneurial endeavors, both the effort required to initiate them and the resistance one normally receives doing business in that context had drastically been cut. Planning and writing and proposing—business processes common to all start-ups—which had formally taken months, now only consumed weeks. And weeks of heretofore cajoling and enrolling partners and investors could now be accomplished in as little as a few days—and even sometimes put to bed in an evening! And these very same strategies worked even faster when I applied them to already functioning business entities.

Small companies who had heard about my work began calling. One of my closest friends had his boss come to see me at a public seminar I was doing in Stockbridge, Vermont, and out of that came my first corporate consult. Out of the results of that consult came another, this time with a rather large local company whose hundred-person sales force was underperforming. In two months I was able to turn that company around. Their sales soared! And so did my reputation. More work followed. Before I knew it, I was working at NLP consultation full time, and having a lot of fun doing it.

I did work for advertisers, weaving NLP technology directly into both radio and television promotions. I trained service company employees to create new levels of rapport with customers. I demonstrated and redefined the phrase "customer service" in the banking industry. For insurance companies, I put highly efficient telephone marketing packages together, using NLP to increase the level of rapport between salesperson and prospective client. In fact, I began initiating different programs that were tailored to the specific needs of each company—from sales, to management, to team building, to leadership, to customer relations, to advertising.

I began doing a lot of television, which brought more

attention to my work. Then, in 1988, I wrote my first book, *Instant Rapport.* Because it became a bestseller, and because I did even more television—shows that included Oprah Winfrey, Sally Jessy Raphael, and Donahue—my work began to get very well known. And the idea for *this* book, on the applications of NLP to business, came directly from people who owned or managed businesses and who would write me and ask if I could take on their firm. Since I obviously can't be everywhere at once, and because a good deal of my time is taken up with national and international work, I wrote this book so that everyone could make use of its incredible new technology.

PEOPLE LIKE PEOPLE WHO ARE LIKE THEMSELVES

The central ingredient that made NLP so effective as a tool for business was its ability to create rapport between people. NLP enables one to become more and more like the person or people with whom one is presently engaged. And for this very reason, people don't have a conscious awareness of its use.

Now, this pleased me but was also a little disconcerting. On the one hand, there was nothing I could demonstrate to people to show off this amazing new skill, and that disappointed me. It wasn't like doing card tricks or showing off a really powerful tennis serve. In essence, it's a process that becomes part of you; you use it as an extension of yourself. On the other hand, because of this very inability to demonstrate it, the process is also quite invisible. Because you're using yourself in a way that mirrors others—and because, by definition, this brings them into rapport with you—*what* you're doing by-passes others' conscious attention. In other words, it's undetectable. When I gave it some thought, I realized how powerful this thing is: the ability to influence people at a deep level of unconsciousness, while apparently doing nothing at all. And accomplishing all this while being in an engaging, open rapport!

The very idea of having a successful business life without being in rapport with others is laughable. Being successful in the business world is obviously a direct function of rapport. It doesn't matter how terrific a product you make or service you offer if you fail at enrolling customers in yourself and hence with your company. Think about it. You are the living representation of your company. How often did you buy, or continue to buy, goods and services from someone with whom you were not in rapport, at least on some level? As a consumer, how often have you turned away from a product because you didn't feel good about the person you were buying it from? As a businessman, how many deals have you lost through the unavailability of rapport? We've all had the experience of wanting—even needing—a product or service, yet avoiding its purchase, or seeking supply at another concern, simply because we didn't like the individual representing the company. Deals involving millions of dollars are predicated on rapport. Interesting, isn't it, this need to like people or feel related to and understood by those we buy from? You'd think companies would understand this and train their representatives appropriately. But oftentimes this isn't the case. After spending tens of millions of dollars on development, marketing, and advertising, these very same companies entrust the selling of their carefully created product to individuals who haven't the slightest notion of what rapport might be, let alone how to produce it.

The point is that in business, as in life, where there is no rapport, there's no sale. Enrolling people in your product or service is the same as enrolling them in you. That's just the way it is.

There have probably been many times in your business life where major events—be they transactions, meetings, or sales efforts—have collapsed simply because you weren't able to close. That's highly understandable. We aren't taught as youngsters to close. We spend part of our lives missing opportunities as a result of either simply fearing them, or of a limited understanding of others' criteria for completion. Unfortunately, ignorance of these facts does not make an acceptable argument for unfavorable results. After entering the business world, you probably began to wonder what it would take to have people understand and agree with your way of doing things. Further, the fantasy of being able to *apply* this ability to your relationship with your boss or client became the stuff of dreams. Given the very nature of our society, the vast majority of us abandoned the hope of realizing this fantasy. It is time to rediscover that miracle—that it does truly exist, and that it's yours for the asking. One must only use a modicum of effort to learn its secrets and become proficient in its use.

As you acquire the skills of NLP, rapidly incorporating them as part of your business resources, you will soon become aware that life at the office has become easier, your relationship with the boss is better, and your ability to close sales has dramatically improved. As a result, before long, your personal income will substantially increase. In a sense, you'll find yourself fully vested in your work. This is because you'll be exerting new control over your business affairs, instead of being a slave to them. You won't have to suffer silently and be a good soldier. Once and for all, you'll be able to push back against those barriers that have kept you in place for so long.

Instead of having to play according your associates' agendas, you'll create your own. People will want to participate in *your* game for a change. You'll receive support for your ideas because they're good. Customers will buy your service or product; and those that already do will buy in larger quantities. Meetings will be a place of opportunity because you'll make them that way. You'll move up the organization. And do you know why all this will be happening to you? The truth is, it's nothing less than *rapport.*

Yes, rapport. That "thing" you've been trying to have with people for as long as you remember.

Rapport.

If you look back on your scattered successes, most always you'll find rapport was present. Sometimes it's hard to see because rapport, like a catalyst in a chemical reaction, doesn't get involved in the mechanics of relating itself. It simply makes relating possible; or more accurately, it creates the probability of relating. In business, when you relate, you sell. Yourself. Your ideas. Your services. Your product. You see, you *are* your product.

When I undertook the writing of this work, I did so with the knowledge that this particular technology had never been successfully explained before. That's why you've probably never heard of it. Certainly its applications to business have remained a closely guarded secret. You'll discover that NLP is one of those terrific surprises in life that comes along all too infrequently. You'll be using its technology—at the beginning somewhat awkwardly, then shortly thereafter fluidly— to make your business life easier, more effective, and more productive. When you have it down, you'll wonder how you ever got along without it.

I *had* to write this book. As if it were some cosmic imperative, I just didn't feel right keeping it to myself. Therefore, on the following pages, you'll make discovery after discovery, and what you'll come away with is the power to be your best. I offer it to you as sorcerer to apprentice, with the unwritten agreement that you'll ethically use this wizardry with integrity and a sense of fairness. With that thought in mind, let's move on and learn the very core of perfect communication: the dynamic power of rapport.

2

HOW RAPPORT CONTROLS

T he application of NLP is extremely powerful. Great care must be exercised to use it ethically.

I've trained tens of thousands of businesspeople and corporations in NLP, and nowhere have I experienced individuals in greater self-examination than in this challenging role. You see, to consistently create rapport with others requires something beyond "technique." It demands the use of something "meta," or above, technique. That's why NLP is often referred to as a meta-model. It is a model of a model. In other words, NLP doesn't play to the conscious mind or the first level of logical thought. Instead, it downloads to lower logical levels with the use of the unconscious mind. Notice I didn't say *through* the use of the unconscious mind. We never try to undermine another's unconscious process by short-circuiting it. Instead, we bend with people's unconscious perceptions, covertly influencing them by being like them. In a sense, we lead them where *we* want to go, down a path with which *they're* familiar. It's a little bit like aikido in that we use our subjects' view of the world as leverage on a road *we* would have *them* naturally choose.

The thrust of industrial NLP is almost entirely dependent on the recognition and acknowledgment that one's subjective experience can be divided into three basic areas of perception, and that rapport is being on the same "wave-length" or having a certain "connection" to another. Specifically, when we're in rapport with others we're seeing things the way they do; we're hearing things as they sound to them; we're even sensing and feeling or responding to a situation as they are. Being in rapport is experiencing life—or a particular perception in life—as though you and another have the same point of view. One can say that both of you operate from the same *model* of the world. It's as though you take in life using the same map of the territory. When you stop and think about it, what could be more natural than having a connection or affinity with someone who sees things just the way you do?

But wait. How many times, statistically, will we actually see things in the same way that others do? Even if we're in rapport, will our judgments and evaluations always match theirs? Hardly. In fact, most of the time, though we may come from the same point of view, our specific values will differ from others'. So obviously we need a better way of creating rapport. And we need a method that will enable us to manipulate this rapport so that we may use it to covertly change another's desires to fit ours. We want to be an architect of opportunity, creating the best possible circumstance for opportunity to occur. In addition, we want to be able to maximize that opportunity so that no matter where we are in the sale, we can instantly close.

A TECHNOLOGY OF RAPPORT

In the best of all possible worlds, consistently finding a common ground with others—a meeting of the minds, as it were—would be achievable at will. It would always provide us with a medium out of which all negotiations would be possible. Instead of spending most of our time trying to talk others into doing what we want, we'd be able to devote ourselves to getting the job done. We'd be home early, spend more time with the family, earn a lot more money, and generally be happier.

Regrettably, the meeting of two minds is a rarity. It's so rare that when we find someone who thinks the way we do and likes the things we like, we tend to promote them, pay them more money, make them our fast friends, even marry them! Such is the power of rapport. Now, if I told you that I had a system that could frame another's experience of you so that they found you to be very much like themselves, and that this in turn made them want to be in agreement with you, what would you think? Would it cross your mind to think about how many different ways and to what results this miraculous wizardry could be used? In how many contexts? The technology of rapport works beautifully to these ends. It allows you to home in on another's criteria for rapport, in much the same way as a heat-seeking missile does, so that you appear to others as though you thought and agreed with whatever *they* consider to be important or highly valued. When this happens, a state of high rapport is created. Once this state is achieved, it is not unlike a highly suggestive trance state, in that people in high rapport are very likely to do the things you want them to do because it's hard for them to reject their mirror image. You can probably sense how important this is in closing deals or working with your boss.

Once upon a time you had this ability at your command, most probably when you were a child. But when we become "socialized," it's programmed out of us, most likely by learning institutions. They teach us to be individuals. We're so busy protecting our own points of view, we never bother to join anyone else's, even for a while. And herein lies an important point: I'm not in any way asking you to give up who you are or what you believe in. I'm not asking you to cease doing those things that make you unique. I encourage you to celebrate your uniqueness, since it's truly a wonderful part of being alive. But what I will ask you to do, from time to time, is to step onto another's high ground, to look down the same telescope, even listen for the same things. And this is where an organized system, or technology, is so important. Without a systemized way of inducing rapport, being like others would simply be a nice thing you do at parties or other functions. Though it might sometimes produce relative states of rapport, what exactly would you do with them? These raw states of rapport would be akin to owning freshly mined diamonds: Without the proper training in diamond refining, what inherent good would they be to you? But if you knew how to refine and cut and polish them, having claim to them might cause your life to be very, very different. I've never thought that simple knowledge is power. It's too raw, and too general. However, *organized* knowledge is something totally different. When we can manipulate raw data and fashion it into a specific technology, then we have something.

In order for us to understand what it is that will so powerfully serve us, we must first take a look at how people subjectively experience reality. If we're to learn anything about NLP and rapport, we must start at the beginning and understand exactly what makes people experience their world in the unique way that they do.

At the start of our lives, when all that we were was just pure warm white light, the only way we had to discriminate in our microcosm was through the symbiotic bond we enjoyed with our parents. As we grew from fetus to infant to young child, we developed our five senses: vision, which allows us to perceive the world of light; audition or hearing, which grants the miracle of sound; kinesthesia or touch, which permits us to feel internally *and* externally; taste or gustation, assigning a unique value to that which we take in and ingest; and smell or olfaction, giving us the ability to discriminate between the odors and scents of life. It is through these receivers—and these receivers alone—that we put together our entire perception of experience.

When we lose a sense, as in the case of blindness or deafness, we are deprived of a critical pathway of experiential information. In effect, we lose a piece of the puzzle. Oftentimes, other senses increase their acuity to make up for the loss of another. An example of this is the blind person who can discriminate between sounds that we can't. Or the deaf person whose eyesight can distinguish between minute lip movements, thereby providing, in a compensatory dynamic, a "makeup" or additional source of information.

In our culture, we've come to value three senses—vision, hearing, and touch—more than taste and smell. But this is not universal. Certain African tribes are more reliant on their sense of taste than on their sense of hearing. And even within a culture, substrates can be found whose sensory inclinations vary. The French are mostly auditory, while Americans tend to be more visual. This is the part that really starts to concern us. The way people take in their world is highly significant because it reveals so much about them.

If you give it some thought, you'll also see that we experience our world not so much by what's out there—because who can actually know what's out there, anyway?—but by our *interpretation* of what's out there. We see, hear, and touch something, and then make a decision about it. The image, sound, and feeling you get in your mind is clearly different than the object you're taking in. For example, when something's yellow, what does that connote? What *is* yellow, anyway? Who assigned the word *yellow* to that particular wavelength of photons? No, it's not the name or the color or the way something feels that gives it meaning to us; it's the way it's set up in our mind that defines it. It's the way we *represent* the great "out there" to ourselves that gives us our experience. From the data coming through our senses we make a *representation* of our experience. It's like a Western Union operator receiving a message in Morse code. Observationally, all he really hears is a beeping noise. But when he represents it to himself, it makes sense because of a template in his mind that gives meaning to the dots and dashes in order to form a word. But what he experiences is not a word. It's a representation of a word.

We experience everything in our lives as though we were sending and receiving Morse code. Our three major senses, or *representational systems,* code all incoming data and translate or decode it at the level of our cerebral cortex. So we get a representation of some event that's taking place in the world. If it's a football game, we get a representation of a football game. If it's a romantic encounter, we get a representation of a romantic encounter. If it's a client's or boss's point of view, we get a representation of that as well. The whole ball of wax is just one huge representation of something that's going on out there in the great "is."

It's probably now occurring to you that everything you experience is just your representation of some drama whose script is already defined, and of which you are merely a player—a walk-on, if you will. You're correct! Our individual notions of reality are just that—individual notions.

This is both bad and good.

It's bad because as a collective species, we can never know the truth about ourselves. We don't know where we come from, or who brought us here, or even why we exist in the first place. I think that is why we fight so much. We don't have the slightest idea of our purpose. We pretend we do by giving ourselves missions and assignments as though we really do have a manifest destiny, but in fact, we don't know—indeed, we cannot know—the truth. The only truth we can ever have is our individual truths. Really, the truth is simply a representation of a belief we hold to be self-evident. In the cosmic dice game of life, we can eternally argue—but never know—what the truth is. And in a large sense, no one will ever win that argument. Unless, of course, we agree to agree on a particular singularity as truth. But obviously this too will simply be a representation of an agreement to agree.

On the other hand, it's this very inability to understand the nature of our experience that so elegantly assists us in creating rapport. Because we're unable to attend to that which is outside our direct experience, much less know its intrinsic truth, there exists a true "blind spot," upon which rests opportunity. Making use of this area that lies beyond our consciousness is precisely the mechanism that supports the creation of rapport. Even more than that, it's necessary. Business rapport depends on using these sensory blind spots to be effective. How else would it be possible for one disparate and autonomous individual to be like another while still maintaining his or her individuality? You see, rapport is generated when two separate individuals share the same map of the territory. That is to say, when we see things in the same way as someone else, we fall into a neurological sameness or congruity which in turn makes us seem very likable to another. This goes far beyond simply liking someone because they agree with you. In fact, when we're in a deep state of rapport with someone, it's often very possible to *disagree* with what they're saying, yet not only stay on the same level of connection, but also bring them into an unconscious agreement with us. Covert rapport technology literally depends on this ability to share or code an experience in the same way as another's.

If we could find a way, then, to jump on the same wavelength as someone else, we'd have a high probability of influencing that person in a deeply persuasive way. The question now begs: Okay, specifically how do I go about being on someone's exact wavelength? And once I'm there, how do I shape the resulting rapport to influence that person in a way that will be beneficial to me?

I think it's terrific that you saw fit to ask, because the rest of this book is targeted at answering that specific question.

NLP is essentially about two major parameters involving rapport:

1. The creation or establishment of rapport.
2. The covert manipulation of it.

To that end, the NLP technology we'll be using is most effective. In the first place, it will allow you to engage almost anyone in an active ongoing rapport. This will immediately shift other people's perspectives of you in a most positive way. You see, one of the key skills of rapport we'll be learning is *mirroring*. Mirroring is simply the process by which we offer the behavior of others directly back to them. This is a simple but very effective way to make use of another's blind spot. But the process of mirroring is really a terrific metaphor for what the rest of NLP does: It gets people to experience you as a subconscious mirror of themselves. While these people will interact with you much as they do now—and little of the pleasure of this give and take will change—the *results* of this interaction will be highly skewed—*in your favor.*

In the second place, NLP will empower you with a technology to manipulate the relationships you have with people so that instead of being at the effect of that relationship, you'll be at the cause of it. When you meet with a client or your boss, rather than being an impotent bystander or at best just one half of the communication process, your input will have the newly found ability to literally finesse the outcome of the transaction. The most thrilling part of the whole process is that the result you get will be almost entirely up to you. In other words, you will be able to create an outcome that's more tailored to your needs. So the next time you're in a committee meeting or selling your product or service, instead of being in a state of hope, you'll be projecting a sense of certainty. That's an interesting point, by the way. Research reveals that people buy from or agree with those who seem to be certain about what they're saying. So if you are truly in alignment with what it is you're trying to get across—and you use the technology of NLP—your chances of actually closing improve from that of random chance, or fifty-fifty, to a positive outcome ratio of about eighty-twenty! That's right. Eight out of ten people you engage while using NLP will conform to an outcome consistent with your intentions.

In the next sections of this book I'm going to talk in some depth about the three distinct classes of representational business types. Some of you may be familiar with them, others not at all. The reason they need to be studied is that in order to use the technology part of NLP, one has to be able to define people by the way they experience their own personal reality.

The remainder of the book is devoted to a thorough and complete explanation of industrial NLP technology. You will find that reading the material in the order in which it's presented will add immensely to your understanding of NLP and to your ability to hold dominion in your business life through its effective use.

3

VISUALLY ORIENTED CLIENTS AND COLLEAGUES

For the 55 percent or so of those of us in business whose primary representational system is visual, much of life's experience is coded and patterned through the eyes. You might say that visuals have a lock on the way the rest of us must get from here to there, as they've very neatly created a world where nearly all we do and affect is oftentimes the result of visually perceived stimuli. As curious as this may seem, there's no clear-cut reason exactly why this is so. I've theorized that it's a learned behavior, probably having its origins in our early childhood. Some theorists believe it has something to do with sight's inherent natural dominance, or a proclivity in our instinctual reactive nature to our environment. Lovely thoughts all, I'm sure, but nonetheless unimportant for our purposes. Suffice to say that visuality is the dominant representational system of our culture.

Many people at the office are visual, and so it's very important for you to be able to delineate what representational area your associates and clients are operating from. That's the reason we'll be spending some time in this chapter describing the visually oriented individual.

<< >>

Visual people are generally more animated and mobile than others. They like movement because it makes sense to them. And when I say "makes sense," I mean that literally: Those perceptions having the widest and deepest effect on these people are those which are coded—"spoken"—in visual language, metaphor, and movement. Visual people are able to code visual reality quicker and with greater ease than auditory people. At this point, it should start to occur to you that if you employ a visual secretary, you wouldn't want to depend on this person's sense of *hearing* to understand you. Can you get a sense of how little spontaneous rapport there can be between an auditory boss and a visual secretary?

One of the very first things to notice about people is the way they relate to the world. The way visual people behave is directly related to what they see. If you put a visual manager into a room that's painted a dark color, you'll likely produce an individual who is depressed most of the business day and whose performance will be greatly reduced. If you give your visual clients the benefits of your product or services solely in the spoken word, your statistics for closing will be a disaster. Likewise, if your boss is a kinesthetic—someone who relates to the world through the way he feels—and you ask him for a raise using charts and graphs of your sales figures, forget about it. You'll be speaking two separate languages.

Visual people code their experience visually. However, that doesn't mean their other senses or representational systems are dormant. Visual people use their secondary senses of hearing and touch to complement what their primary representational system communicates to them, thereby giving them a more complete picture of what's happening out there. As we'll soon learn, being "primarily visual" simply means that we perceive reality—a good deal of the time—visually. The key phrase here is *a good deal of the time.* That's because even the most visual of us still depend on our other, or secondary, senses.

We all—visuals and nonvisuals alike—share visual quali-
ties. We need to. For instance, I'm a true auditory, but my
strategy—my exact formula—for car buying is visual. When
I go shopping for a new car, what matters most for me is the
way it looks. If it fails my visual criteria, it wouldn't matter
if the car could traverse hyperspace or get a hundred miles
to the gallon. I'd just as soon pass. If the car salesman doesn't
understand this particular trait of mine, he's wasting his time
with me. No matter how he carries on about the sound of the
motor or feel of the engine—even about the "rich Corinthian
leather"—it won't close a sale. At least not approached that
way. But if he can determine that I'm an auditory with a
visual car-buying strategy, well, that's another story.

So who is the visual? What does she look like? How can we
identify visuals so as to be in rapport and influence them?

Visuals have a strong impact simply because there are so
many of them in business. To begin with, most of the world
we live in is mapped out by visuals. (This is a cultural bias,
as people from other countries may not be quite so visual.
For example, the French are mostly auditory, while the Sovi-
ets are primarily kinesthetic.) All those signs, and maps, and
designer colors, and wonderful architecture are the products
of people who are primarily visual.

Often visuals are quick to speak and don't have much
patience. Most everything they think is made available to
them in the form of pictures. That's the way they code reality.
Research indicates that those who think in pictures think
quicker than those who think in words or feelings. That
doesn't mean visuals are smarter; it means that visuals *see*
what you mean rather quickly. In turn, they're usually ready
for more information sooner than others may be. If there's
anyone in your life who you think is impatient, it's a good bet
that person processes his experience visually. Because of the
way pictures flip through their consciousness, visuals tend to
try to get out as much information as possible. They always
communicate as quickly as possible before they lose the

image. Therefore, they hate to be interrupted. It cuts them off from their train of thought and frustrates them—a good deal more so than it does others.

Creating rapport with visuals is not difficult. They love validation of visual thought. Repeating the last sentence or the last few words of a discourse while actively listening to a visual really engages him. But always be careful not to mimic.

You must understand the position you're in when interacting with a visual. Because visuals require more attention, you can't be as laid back and comfortable as you can be with others. Avoid asking them to get a feeling about something. Avoid conveying information to them with dramatic overtones. Using secondary representational systems is something they haven't got time for. But asking them to picture something will actively begin the process of persuasion.

Unlike auditories and kinesthetics, visuals tend to use their hands a great deal when talking. These *gestural cues* represent the outline of their thinking. Visual bosses will often speak with their hands, especially when they get passionate about what they're communicating. That's because they can see what they're talking about as they speak. They form an image of the thought—a picture, if you will. Those of you who are visual have used images as you've read this. Especially the part where I asked you to recall a conversation that you once had. Visuals even recall their feelings as a picture. They'll see themselves feeling bad or good as an image in their mind.

Take a good look at a classic visual, George Bush. The man simply cannot talk without his hands. He speaks in relatively short bites. His process words are visual. He hates being interrupted. His brain works through so many pictures that he often garbles his words and gets impatient. The president, however, does check his images kinesthetically. He tries to get a sense of the issue as well as a picture of it. One can clearly see this in his news conferences.

To give you a better understanding of how visuals appear in business, I'm going to outline them in their typical roles.

THE VISUAL BOSS

Here's a man or woman whose response to the working environment is, "Let me see it." Their sense of vision is everything to them. Long talks, emotional pleas, and lengthy meetings strongly work against your relationship with the visual. It's not that he's truly impatient; it's just that his mind sorts his experience by what he sees, not by what he hears or feels. The visual boss would rather you show him your work than tell him about it.

He's usually pretty mobile, walking from here to there, speaking in short thoughts and often telling you to give him the bottom line. If ever there's a person who's result-oriented, it's him. The visual boss will run from this thought to that, trying to form mini-opinions as he sorts out his agenda. He will try to elicit responses from staff in a way he can visually understand. When he's able to get those representationally coded responses, he's happy—even if the news itself isn't that great. What bothers him is a continual barrage of information that is rapportless. In this case, that means lacking visual description. For example:

BOSS: Where's the Bloomingdale account? Anybody see it?

MANAGER: I have a feeling it's in the conference room.

BOSS: What do you mean? Didn't you look?

MANAGER: I wasn't handling that account. I didn't sense it would need my attention.

35

Boss: Really. Well, next time why don't you try opening your eyes? Maybe it would be good for business. Get the picture?

Do you notice what's going on here? The manager is responding in a way that frustrates his boss. He's talking about his feelings because he's probably a kinesthetic. However, the boss wants a visual response. That's what he needs in order to make sense out of the situation. Take a look at the next example and notice the difference when the manager simply responds visually.

Boss: Where's the Bloomingdale account? Anybody see it?

Manager: I think I saw it in the conference room.

Boss: Terrific. What's it doing there?

Manager: I couldn't get a good perspective of what was needed, so I asked someone else if they might focus in on it and get back to me with a clearer picture.

Boss: Oh. Then let's move on.

Knowing which representational system your boss comes from can make a very big difference in your working life. If you have a visual boss, that difference is a critical one.

The visual boss can be easy to work for if you know what she needs to experience in order to notice you. For instance, telling her your wonderful ideas about a project or a client, or anything that causes more than ten or fifteen seconds of conversation, will turn her off. That's right. In the main, lengthy discourses, no matter how right you are, won't carry that much weight. It just doesn't compute. On a very deep and intimate level, it's just not intelligible to her.

You know that expression she puts on her face? You

know, the one that says, "I'm on the beach in Bali, and even though you're telling me something you consider really important, I don't particularly care?" Well, that's because you're talking word salad. Usually, if you interact with her like this enough times, she'll be anchored to you as someone who may very well be smart, attractive, and part of the local scenery, but mostly you'll be thought of as just another irritant that she has to put with. I wonder how many times you've heard her say something like "Doesn't anybody see what I mean?" or "Can't you picture what I'm trying to show you?" and tossed those remarks off with not even a thought. If you take a good look at it, you'll see what I mean.

Visual bosses love graphs. They love presentations. Brief presentations. Presentations that visually show them what you would like to tell them. You know the expression: A picture is worth a thousand words. Well, keep that in mind when you talk with your visual boss.

A short while ago, I had the opportunity to consult with the vice president of a famous brokerage house. He wanted to know what I could do to help them improve their in-house communications. Well, just because I knew I could help didn't necessarily mean *he* knew I could. I had to make sure he'd have that revelation within his own experience. Since I knew NLP, it was no effort at all to ascertain that he was visual; and that being the case, I simply communicated with him on his wavelength—a visual wavelength. What did this look like? For one thing, I spoke quicker and got to the point faster. For another, I made sure to use my visual presentation package. This includes pictures, graphs, charts, and even a video that supports my oral communication. When you are thoughtful enough to code your presentation so that other people can get a clear experience of what you want them to know, oftentimes you simply need not go any further. You are completely understood.

In one sense, you don't have to work too hard with a visual boss. That's because visuals tend to judge your work more on how it looks and less on what it produces. Visuals are not easy to fool, but you can get more mileage with less effort as long as it looks like you're busy. When I was in graduate school, we had a professor of diagnosis who was totally visual, and he made it very clear to all of us that if we expected to get a high grade, it simply wasn't enough to know the material. He conveyed to us, nonverbally, that demonstration of one's ability was all-important. To a large extent, it didn't matter if we could "talk" the material or not, as long as we visually demonstrated it. We drew graphs; we scurried about with this chart and that sheet; some of us even drew pictures of our opinions on the blackboard for him. The point is that those who succeeded visually did better than those who were unable to comply with his visual cues. I said *unable* because to those of us who were auditory and kinesthetic, all that running around made no sense. It didn't compute. We were out of rapport with our professor.

A last word about working for a visual. Don't automatically assume that they like flashy things. You must ascertain, through observation, exactly *how* your boss is visual. You'll find out rather quickly. Some visuals like bright things; others need soft and muted images. You'll know exactly how to please him or her once you've opened your eyes.

THE VISUAL CLIENT OR CUSTOMER

As complicated as the visual boss is, that's how easy the visual buyer or client is. You just have to know what to do. Such buyers have one rule you must comply with if you're interested in making a sale, and that's "Show me." Don't waste your time talking with them, because it's pointless—unless you're describing a picture or an image.

I'm fascinated by watching salespeople in department stores "sell" their various products. Half the time these people couldn't care less about the sale. The rest of the time they fire "buckshot." That's the term I use for selling clients when you don't know what you're doing. Just put it out there and if it works, terrific. If it doesn't, oh well, there's always tomorrow. This is how a lot of people in the selling profession work. Of course, that also explains why truly successful salespeople are so hard to find.

About one person in a thousand uses her natural ability to sell. That's right, just one in a thousand. She's the person who does all the business. Whether she's a retail salesperson or the regional manager, wherever she goes, sales follow because she has the ability to generate rapport. When she's homing in on a prospect, she starts to become just like the person she's selling. Most of the time she isn't consciously aware of this. Few people are. But somewhere inside her, she bonds to the client in a way others are not able to.

To begin with, let the visual look for as long a time as he needs to. This is important because the sale will be predicated on the look of the product. This also applies to any service you might provide. When you sense he's ready, ask questions that stimulate visual pictures, such as:

"How do you think that will look on you?"
"Can you see yourself using this at home?"
"Have you ever pictured yourself looking that good?"

This forces the client to consult his visual remembered or constructed pictures. Either way, you've put him on the right road—*his* road—so that he may come to a decision.

Visual clients will oftentimes be harried and in a rush to get somewhere. Let them be rushed! It's their way of deciding. Cut them the widest possible berth you can. If they look undecided, you might ask:

"Is there anything else I could show you?"
or
"Would you like to look at our catalog?"

or
"I can show you a picture of the product so that you
might have a better look at it. Would you mind?"

More often than not, visuals will try to see how something looks in a physical way. For instance, if they're buying
a shirt, they'll hold it up in front of them and look in the
mirror to confirm or reject their physical picture. Or, say, if
they're buying a car, they'll need to sit in the car or look at
someone else sitting in the car to reach a decision. More
closings are lost by a salesperson's ignorance of visual sam-
pling than anything else except price.

A chain of computer stores retained me once to diagnose
and treat their slow sales rate. Almost immediately I noticed
that there were no sensory cues available for customers to
hook on to. The salespeople spoke in monotones, the computers had no literature stacked beside them picturing the computer at work, and finally, it was very difficult to come away
with a positive feeling about the stores or the computers
themselves, because they didn't have a "high-touch" presence
to them—you just didn't feel good about buying one. They
looked terrific, and the salespeople were attentive enough,
but it was hard to picture yourself competently using one of
their computers. It was apparent to me that they needed a
visual representation that would convince people they themselves "fit" well with the stores' products.

I tried a little experiment. I told the president of the
company to install mirrors in each store in such a way that
people sitting down could glance at themselves working on
the computers. I didn't try to manipulate the other two varia-
bles of hearing and touch. I just wanted to provide a lot of
visual input for prospective clients. Within a month, the mirrors were installed at five of the company stores.

Four weeks later we took a look at the sales statistics, and
sure enough, they rose about 15 percent. And that was with

only one representational system enhanced. I completed the consult by changing their auditory and kinesthetic parameters as well. By the end of the project, sales had improved by an astounding 29 percent!

In one respect, visual customers or clients are easier than either the auditory or kinesthetic customers. Once they complete their decision strategy, they go right for the buy. If you access them correctly, it will be a rather quick sale. If you have friends who are "shopaholics," the probability of them being visual is quite high. If they're not primary visuals, then you'll find their *strategy* for buying is visual. I have a friend who's a total kinesthetic. This man's life is wrapped around his emotions. Whatever else he does, he always judges the result by how it makes him feel. However, this man's strategy—*his particular behavior when performing specific tasks*—for buying is visual. So when he enters a car showroom he switches from his primary representational system—kinesthetic—to total visual. That translates to a very feeling individual who goes through a major representational change while shopping.

This isn't unusual. Everyone has specific strategies for performing specific behaviors. The trick is to be able to discover the particular strategy they use for that behavior, and acquire it. Once you know someone's strategy for something, it's a forgone conclusion that you'll be able to manipulate the interaction between the two of you. And once you've done that, they literally *have* to buy what you're selling!

There are a few physical manifestations that are indigenous to the visual client, and you would do well to learn them. In my line of work, I depend on the nonverbal even more than the verbal. People are constantly communicating with us even though their lips might never move. I'm not talking about body language. Body language connotes that there's meaning behind this movement or that grimace. That's a whole other story and really not appropriate for our purposes. Besides, in NLP we don't look for the *meaning* of behavior so much as we use a particular piece of physical evidence to *mirror,* so that we become more like the person we want to influence. See the chapter on mirroring.

Visual customers invariably breathe high in the chest, and their respiration is often shallow. If you ask a visual customer a question and look closely as he answers, you may notice him literally stop breathing as he accesses an image or picture to see the appropriate answer. Visual people see themselves in the pictures of their answers. Sometimes you'll notice that visuals lose a little color in their faces as they scan for an answer.

The visual client may have an expressive voice that speaks of the urgency to complete a thought before the image vanishes. That's why visuals cannot be cut off easily. If you have a friend or acquaintance who never yields to you in a conversation, smart money would say that person's a visual. He tries to persevere because once the visual thought is gone, so goes his train of thought. You can probably see how this could work to his disadvantage in a court of law.

I have a client who is the managing partner of a very prestigious law firm. He came to me for a consultation regarding the cross-examination of a witness in appellate court, hoping to get a previous decision set aside. When I actually observed the witness on a redirect a week later, I could see that he was strongly visual. Because I was going on an overseas business trip two days later, I couldn't spend as much time as I would have liked arming my client with NLP technology. So I simply told him to cut the witness off as much as he could and not give him enough time to form a thought-image for an answer. In other words, be as intrusive as possible within the confines of the situation. This, I ex-plained, would impede the witness's recall and thus under-mine his credibility, swaying the judge in the direction of my client.

My client won the litigation before the next day's recess.

I'm going to relegate the valuable information that eye accessing cues provide us to the chapter devoted exclusively to them. Let me just introduce you to the idea now by telling you that members of each of the representational systems use their eyes in different scanning patterns. When we learn about them, you'll be astounded by how much you can alter your relationships with important clients or customers just by reading their eye movements.

THE VISUAL SECRETARY

This above all: Show her what you want her to do.

Visual secretaries are, in the main, powerful allies. They have a picture in their minds of exactly how this or that should be. If you let this person know what you want done—in visual language—he will perform mightily. These people are incredibly efficient and will go way beyond the call of duty as long as they get a clear picture of the way things should be.

They learn by observation. You're better off *showing* him how you like things than *telling* him. If you want him, for example, to put a report together for the end of the week, show him an example of one that's already completed and ask him to use that as a template. He'll astound you! How-ever, if you make the mistake of *describing* the same task to him—especially in other than visual terms—you'll often find the result will be *his* conception of what *he* thinks looks right.

Visual secretaries often dress in a manner that reflects their internally generated feelings. When they're centered, when their finger is on the pulse and they're not bogged down by emotional images inconsistent with a good demeanor, visuals will tend to dress on the bright side. Conversely, when they are preoccupied with personal matters and when their thoughts are scattered, you'll notice them dressing incongruently. By that I mean either dressed down in color or dressed somewhat asymmetrically. My favorite example of this is the noted psychologist and total visual Joyce Brothers, who ordinarily clothes herself in well-arranged bright pastels. However, when I've observed her in situations that would cause anxiety, her clothes were more muted and haphazardly worn. This can be a terrific behavioral cue in assisting you in exerting influence with visual people. When they dress down, the best way to effect rapport is to come down with them— even if that means showing up for an important meeting attired in the same general manner as they. Likewise, if your visual boss or secretary is put together well, you'll know that you can't make yourself heard if your presentation is anything other than high-toned, to the point, and sharp.

If you are into charts and graphs and presentations, the visual secretary will shine. She's a terrific public relations agent and is oftentimes considered to be very effective, if slightly impatient, with people. When she's on, she'll dazzle your clients. If she works with a computer, by all means get her one that has a good graphical interface, like a Macintosh.

The visual secretary will be loyal as long as life at the office looks good to her. When her picture of loyalty is broken, when she can't see beyond her considerations, she'll be open to change. In fact, because of her visuality, this will be quite apparent to you—if you know what to look for. If she is considering leaving, her language will be chock-full of visual images subconsciously addressing this situation. For example, her analogies and metaphors will tend to rest on visual descriptions of change and new beginnings. Her dressing may take on a sudden shift of presentation. She may start rearranging her desk or buy little doodads that brighten up her work space.

Visuals make good secretaries because they execute their missions deftly. They're not that great on the phone, however, and really dislike someone who can't get to the point quickly. That's one reason customer relations is not the job for them. Interestingly, you'll want to give her a raise or promotion because she'll look like she's working hard. And visuals *are* hard workers. But be careful, and check to see how thorough her work is. Once a project looks like it's pretty close to completion, she'll be off and running, often leaving you with loose ends. Always show her what a completed project looks like. Then you're set.

Because I'm in a service business and the people who call me usually have definite feelings about how they want their company to run, I made sure my secretary is kinesthetic with an auditory communication strategy. She solves a lot of my problems because she understands both my scheduling difficulties and the problems my clients have. In my line of work, confidentiality is everything, so my secretary is very sensitive to this problem. In fact, she's so feeling-oriented that by the time I make contact, a good portion of my job is handled. She also communicates auditorily, so her phone work is superb. For me, she's the best of all possible choices. However, if your work is about anything visual—if it has anything to do, for example, with art, movies, entertainment, photography, magazines, decorating, architecture, fashion, or travel—by all means hire a visual.

4

AUDITORY CUSTOMERS AND MANAGERS

'm auditory. Practically everything I do is based upon how something sounds.

Auditories tend to work in places where they have a soothing background. They don't function well when placed in environments that are sonically overwhelming. In this respect they differ from visuals, who can endure a lot more visual static than anybody else.

Auditories have a terrific capacity for handling people. They do wonderfully well in customer relations. I consulted with one particular government agency that prides itself on its relationship with the public. When I went in to fine tune their advertising, I found, not to my surprise, that over 55 percent of their agents were auditories. Even more interesting is the fact that of the ninety people handling the public relations department, fully half had tested with practically no visual skills for communications. This is significant if only for the fact that most companies have set up their customer liaison division very visually; and most of these are entirely dependent on visual cues to keep the continuity. According to a majority of Fortune 1,000 CEOs, no contingency is set up to account for the dollar differences in representational dysfunction. And that's just a fancy way of saying that people are selected for jobs without ever discriminating for how they communicate.

<< >>

Auditories are extremely open to both sides of an argument, even if they find out they're not right. Since their world—their representational reality—is based on sound, they discriminate largely by the spoken word. The way they make decisions is also based primarily on spoken logic. I'm referring to verbalization from without *and* within. Auditories always compare how something should be done by the way it "fits" in their aural syntax. They converse with themselves on both levels of consciousness, sometimes moving their lips unintentionally in the process. They are always in a state of discussion. That's the way they make sense of their experience. You might say that auditories process their experience by the use of dialogue. When an auditory thinks, she thinks in language. So, for the most part, ideas are represented to her—in her mind—as conversations. When you ask her to make a decision about something, she'll no doubt create a two-sided internal conversation in an attempt to resolve the challenge. When we learn about eye accessing cues in Chapter 7, you'll be able to physically see this process by the way auditories move their eyes as they process linguistic thought.

One of the negative aspects of encountering an auditory in business is the tendency of some auditories to try to dominate conversations. Because they don't maintain their train of thought as well as kinesthetics do, and probably as a result of their never-ending process of auditory thought, these people may push too hard when explaining something.

Auditories are primarily sound-oriented, but they, like all of us, possess the other representational senses. People just tend to use one of them more than others. That's why I call these dominant senses *primary* representational systems. If you're an auditory, that means that your primary representational system is auditory. If you're visual, your primary representational system is vision. And for kinesthetics the primary representational system is their feeling states.

All of us, however, have secondary representational systems that we use for specific behaviors or tasks. I mentioned in the last chapter that I'm primarily a true auditory, but my strategy—my exact formula—for car buying is visual. When I go shopping for a new car, what matters most for me is the way it looks. Well, in addition to that, I also have specific behaviors—or strategies, as I call them—that are feeling-oriented, or kinesthetic. One particular strategy that I use that is obviously flawed is my kinesthetic strategy for navigation. Because I do a lot of consulting, television, and seminar work, I travel a lot. And I enjoy the actual traveling part. However, because my navigation behavior is kinesthetic, once I get off the plane, I unfortunately tend to get lost rather quickly. That's because I judge my whereabouts by the way the surroundings *feel* to me. For instance, when I'm on my way to the office, I know I'm on the right track because I feel a certain assurance from my surroundings. And when I'm home, in the countryside of New York, this strategy works. But—*for me*—this strategy is kinesthetically flawed, because when I'm on the road, I constantly get lost. As you can plainly see, some strategies are better than others. What I'm trying to convey to you is that though we primarily represent experience through one dominant representational system, we also use our other or secondary representational systems as well; and certain strategies of behavior are more efficient and elegant than others. This is something we'll learn to use to our advantage as we learn the finer distinctions of NLP.

Since auditories are so in tune with the sounds around them, it goes without saying that ordinary background noise that most people don't pay much attention to is often a real source of discomfort to auditories. One of the first things I do when I consult with companies is to review what kind of acoustical environment they provide. Six times out of ten, the background noise is a huge distraction to auditory employees—not to mention auditory customers. Statistics confirm this. Usually 21 percent of the employees—almost the exact proportion of the auditory population—get nauseated, dizzy, or come down with stomach cramps or other uncomfortable symptoms directly as a result of what I call sonic assault. The first thing I do is manipulate the background noise so that it provides a pleasing and productive zone in which people can work. In one particular long-distance company I worked with, I engineered a tape which so effectively altered the workplace that almost immediately productivity dramatically rose. The company slashed absenteeism by 18 percent! The employees felt much better about their working environment and, of course, revenues went up.

With many firms there is such an incredible amount of psychological ignorance regarding employees and customers that just manipulating *any* of the work space results in some kind of revenue improvement. You can't expect to run a company efficiently when you haven't taken into consideration how your people run their reality. Often I meet managers who think I'm going to perform voodoo rights on their workers and clients and suddenly everything will be all right. The truth is, half the time I never get to the great stuff—like phonological ambiguities, belief and value torque, representational advertising, or activating clients' buying strategies— because there's so much housekeeping to get done. A lot of the time, I spend only two or three days adjusting some basic parameters like sales and telephone scripts, and that's all it takes! When they ask me to bring in the heavy artillery, I tell them to call me in a month or two when the dust settles. And you know what? They want even more. They get power crazy. Except this isn't some kind of far-out wizardry. It's simply reaching people on the level of their subjective experience and using that conduit to create powerful results.

<<>>

Auditory businesspeople are a graceful lot, and you can depend on them to get the job done, *if* it's explained to them.

The key here—as if you don't already know—is to *tell* them what you want done. Don't bother writing it down and sending an interoffice memo. That would be like telling a visual boss you want to read him a review of the weekly sales record. Or trying to make him smile by sharing with him how secure you feel about the weekly numbers. You'd get about as far as one paragraph before he'd mentally go for a stroll in the park because you didn't SHOW him the darn numbers! Well, if you carry the same logic over to auditories, you'd know you have to TELL the auditory what you want or expect from her, and get your point across in verbal communication. Auditories thrive on the spoken word; put it to good use.

Studies indicate that auditories generally like to listen to information at about the same rate as they speak. Use this to your advantage when you communicate with them. Additionally, they respond very well to diction that's anything but monotone. If you vary your inflection, timbre, cadence, intonation, and pitch, it will be greatly appreciated, though I don't mean you have to go through all this to be understood. I do mean that varying these aural parameters will make the creation of rapport much easier, therefore getting the job done quicker and with more accuracy. What I've learned about dealing with large groups of auditories is that they will serve you very well with only the smallest bit of information, as long as it is delivered in a way that they can understand.

If I had to pick one area where auditories are at the top of their voice, it would be customer relations. Their level of productivity just soars here because these people are truly in their own medium. Any areas in which auditories are left to depend on their skills of communication are usually the areas they excel. However, this quite naturally depends on how they are trained.

We tend to excel to the degree that we have the tools of the medium in which to excel. Or put another way:

PEOPLE DO THE BEST THEY CAN WITH THE RESOURCES THEY HAVE

If we place auditories in jobs that require strong visual resources or states, like bookkeeping or designing, they will most likely be frustrated and therefore may unconsciously sabotage the work. This isn't because these individuals are stupid or lazy; it's simply because they're being utilized in the wrong way. Someone forgot to read the manufacturer's directions. I can't tell you how often this is the case. One must be scrupulous in placing or matching the right person with the right job. And the way to do this, of course, is to test for representational type. Once this is known, not only will job efficiency double, but most people will actually enjoy their work. More about this later in the chapter on strategies.

Auditories are physically different than visuals. This is probably the result of using specific types of auditory accessing phenomena throughout their life. Much the same way as we have different ways of walking that result from lifelong physical habits, we also mold behavioral traits that present themselves as outward expressions of our unique representational type.

Because of the way auditories access sound, their breathing reflects a steady rhythm and clarity. Unlike visuals, auditories pull their breaths from the lower diaphragm, for a more mobile way of breathing. It's more relaxed.

When auditories sigh, you can be pretty sure they've just had some major dialogue with themselves. If you're selling an auditory client, and you want him to reach a decision point so that you know where to proceed, simply ask him to *listen* to the good points about the product or service. When he brings up an objection, you can do one of two things. You can tell him that they're not worth talking about. This may actually work, but it may also frustrate him. Or you can use his very "auditoriness" to reframe the objections within his buying strategy. This is powerful stuff because, in a very large sense, you're following his exact blueprint for buying. And in so doing, you are greatly enhancing the probability of a sale. And also, since this technique is so profound, it literally dispenses with our old notions of buyer's remorse. When you reframe a prospective client's notion of what he wants, you eliminate buyer's remorse because you're not selling him anything other than what he needs. Because you've changed the context of the sale at the outset, you're already in agreement with your client.

More about the use of strategies later on.

Auditories usually aren't as tense or lean as visuals. Nor as tight or muscular as kinesthetics. But because auditories don't demand a lot of touch, you probably won't find them in too many hands-on occupations. You will find them where communication is of primary importance. Auditories make poor assembly line workers. They can sometimes be poor readers. If your boss is an auditory, whatever you do, don't drown him in papcrwork. And don't present your results in some long-winded document. It won't work. But being precise and narrative is greatly appreciated. A metaphor or two is terrific because that's how auditories think. Metaphors actually lubricate the communication process. If you're working in customer relations with an auditory client, be gentle and to the point. Make your words descriptive and clear. Try to match auditory processing words as much as you can. For example:

Mismatched and Out of Rapport

UNHAPPY CUSTOMER: I'm not satisfied with the software program you sold me last week. Its instructions aren't clear, and when I finally get it to talk to me, it doesn't say the right thing. It's confusing. I need help.

UPSET CUSTOMER RELATIONS AGENT: I'm sorry you're having a problem, but no one else has ever had that complaint. Have you really looked over the manual? This program isn't supposed to "talk," sir. Are you sure you're reading the instructions correctly?

UNHAPPY CUSTOMER: I've read the manual until I'm deaf, and it still isn't clear. I know it's not supposed to talk. I meant that figuratively. You know what? I want my money back. Do you understand me now?

Obviously the customer relations agent knows nothing about rapport or he would have immediately picked up the problem. If he knew the customer is an auditory struggling with a representational language problem, he would have easily saved the sale. For example:

Matched and In Rapport

UNHAPPY CUSTOMER: I'm not satisfied with the software program you sold me last week. Its instructions aren't clear, and when I finally get it to talk to me, it doesn't say the right thing. It's confusing. I need help.

CUSTOMER RELATIONS AGENT: Yes, sir, I can hear you're having a difficult time with our product, and I apologize. We have an excellent tutorial on audio-

tape that guides you easily through the entire program. Let me send it to you, at no charge. All that I
ask is that you call me after you receive the tape and
let me know if we're now talking the same language
and if you have any other questions.

SATISFIED CUSTOMER: Thanks so much. I really appreciate your help, and I'll give it a try.

Auditories may ruminate for a long time about a decision that hasn't gone their way. And you must remember that
when you explain something to an auditory, she'll consider
it eight ways from the middle. She'll make fairly complex
business decisions based on the way an idea or concept
sounds. Auditories are able to extract so much more information out of verbal communication that often they'll be ahead
of you—even in an area they know nothing about. Auditories
process language in much the same way as computers process digitized signals. They're very quick. You must keep up
with them if you want to work or sell to them.

THE AUDITORY BOSS

Here's an individual who'll have some sort of acoustical stim-
ulation going on at all times. It could be music; it might be
some sort of machine like a sound soother; or it might simply
be a window kept open to hear the beat of the world. Auditory
bosses don't mind the hum of a computer going full speed.
They whistle, hum, even subvocalize. But not infrequently,
they'll prefer silence. Silence will allow them to sort things
through—especially if things have been rough. Either of these
personality characteristics is common with auditories.

The auditory boss is not terribly interested in the visual
portion of experience. If you communicate with a lot of

charts and graphs, you'll lose him. Rely on the spoken word as much as possible. Because auditories *sort* their experience by sound, any requests, such as those for a raise or promotion, should never be presented in writing, if at all possible. Your auditory boss will understand you much better, and truly get a sense of your worthiness, if you speak to him or her in person.

If you take the time to look, you'll discover how truly easy it is to manipulate the environment so as to produce the results you want. One must always consider that people who sort by sound live by sound. They're comfortable with hearing the results. Feelings, while playing an important part in everyone's life, aren't primarily used in the auditory's experience to make decisions. Key decisions are made by how it sounds to him. Mostly, he'll check with his feelings *after* he decides about something. He or she may be the most sensitive person you know, but when it comes down to reality—their reality—they'll always go by what they hear, be that external input or internal dialogue.

Some auditory bosses may talk you deaf, mute, and blind. They have a hard time being quiet. But they don't mind being conversationally corrected, as long as it's done appropriately. The same holds true for managers. In fact, you may be thanked for helping your boss get back to the point. For example, last year, I completed a huge training with one of the biggest cable television providers in the United States. The problem they had was in public relations. When you called to complain, you got a wordy reception. And it wasn't always that friendly. It turns out that the training director who set up the department was—you guessed it—a visual. Because of this, after a while the customer service operators started sorting out company problems in the same manner as their manager. That is to say, they argued with you until they had their way or you hung up. I know because I made a few dozen calls to them as part of my work-up. Their whole strategy for handling customer complaints was a visual disaster.

And they were truly unhappy with their jobs because they hated arguing. They just hadn't been given any resources for handling company problems other than that of their visual manager. When I retrained them, I had to install a completely different *auditory* methodology for their work. In this particular case, I created an audiotape customer relations script that trained the operators in creating rapport with callers even before dealing with the specific problem at hand. Once rapport was established, the mechanical part of the job became easy. In fact, the operators actually began to enjoy serving the consumers' needs while sticking to company policy. I also requested the visual manager be transferred, and he was, to satellite programming, where his visual skills were greatly needed and appreciated.

If your boss is an auditory, you'll plainly notice how the company bears his mark. Meetings will be more frequent. Reports will be shorter. There'll be a lot more of a "Tell Me" than "Show Me" attitude.

If you want to get a raise, explain to your auditory boss how you deserve it. Use metaphors or stories. Don't forget that auditories think in words and dialogues, and stories are a natural and excellent way to communicate a particular point. Usually the best stories are the ones that representationally lay out your point of view. Using such a metaphor would typically communicate the notion of abundance, giving, and increased responsibility. Anchors, which you'll learn in Chapter 10, will work superbly in this regard. Oftentimes, when I ask for a larger fee, I use the metaphor that sometimes "less expensive is more expensive." And I certainly use metaphors or stories when I'm dealing with auditory training managers. But all these strategies must be couched in an auditory context for them to get positive results. You must orient any conversation with your boss in such a way as to stimulate an internal dialogue within himself. If you don't, he won't get a *motivating* and clear thought of what you want.

One of the best ways to stimulate an auditory boss's thoughts is with questions. Questions provoke transderivational searches that lead an auditory to successful decision making. The trouble is, your boss is rarely asked good questions. Forget about asking him "Why" questions. For his purposes, they're meaningless. If you continue to ask your boss "Why" questions, his brain will come up with answers you may not like. You see, the brain will *always* supply answers—that's what it's designed for. The problem is, a lot of the time the answers are incorrect. The brain has no fail-safe in this; as long as it provides *answers*—correct or incorrect—it's fulfilling its prime directive. In the case of an auditory, this is doubly so. Ask the right questions, get good answers. What are the right questions? Usually those that begin with *"What."* "What can I do to get this done?" or "What can I do to make this happen?" Even "What about a raise?" Obviously that's not all you have to do. You've got to back up your requests with performance. All I'm saying is that why not speak to your boss in a way—in a dialect, if you will—that he'll really understand? You'll find that not only will you get what you want, but believe it or not, you'll actually be in rapport with him.

THE AUDITORY CLIENT OR CUSTOMER

Stop interrupting him, and let him talk! I don't care if you're bored to death. That's not the point. If you want to be in rapport with him, if you want to close the deal, stay cool and listen. The auditory client is a piece of cake if you just pay attention to what he's saying. Sandwiched in-between all that word salad, there's a pretty obvious buying strategy.

It's like buried treasure, just waiting for you to pluck.

Auditories talk more than others. They need to do this in order to make their own thoughts more complete. They scan laterally left to right with their eye accessing cues, searching for sounds that sccm appropriate to the current situation. They *ask* to be sold. If you don't give them enough information, they'll come right out and ask you for it. Don't ignore this telltale sign. Don't be afraid to keep selling. Auditories will let you know when they've heard enough by speaking up or cutting you off. Another way of recognizing auditories is by their lip movements. When you're on their wavelength, auditories will oftentimes move their lips in time to what you're saying. They subvocalize. If they're in this mode, stay with them. When they stop mirroring your speech, they've digested the thought. Move on from there.

Whatever it is you're selling, let the auditory customer hear it. If it's a vacuum cleaner, turn it on. If it's computers, load in one of those guided tour diskettes and let him drink in the sound. If you're selling cars, let her hear the sound of the door slamming, and how great the sound system performs—and go ahead and beep the horn! That's what she wants. That's what she needs. She'll love it.

I've recently been retained by a major financial services company in an effort to assist them in creating higher sales. I'm excited about this project because we're using videotape in what I call "biased representations" to make the sale appealing. It works like this: When a prospective client walks in, the account executive will determine whether he or she is visual, auditory, or kinesthetic. Depending on which representational type they are, that's the videotape they'll be shown. In the visual tape, the client will be accessed through his sense of vision, seeing the product do its job. In the auditory tape, the client will be accessed through how the program sounds. And with kinesthetics, they'll be treated to a tape that makes them feel particularly good about the company and be brought in touch with how much they *need* the product. The goal is leveraged persuasion through the unconscious process of rapport. Am I at all making sense?

There is something you should look out for when selling an auditory. His companion. Auditories tend to bring along another person, if at all possible, when faced with large decisions. When they have a pal or spouse or relative along with them, it can be a real challenge. Contending with your auditory's own dialogue is very demanding, but when there's another person along, it will stimulate more inner dialogue within the auditory client. At best, this will be a distraction. At worst, it can kill a deal right on the spot. That's not only bad for you, it's also bad for them. Auditories get talked out of more things—oftentimes things they really need—by friends and relatives than any other type. If it's possible, try to separate them. Or *break* rapport with the companion long enough to engage your customer effectively.

In one very big respect, prospective auditory clients are the easiest to sell. They're easy because they are receptive to the most obvious kinds of verbal communication. Your choices are wide open as to how you want to influence them. You can rely on your natural sense of selling, your verbal presentation. You won't have to worry about visual images or about internal feelings. You're already geared up in this respect, so simply applying the techniques of NLP to what seems natural and to what you already know should, in the auditory's case, be a simple matter.

THE AUDITORY SECRETARY

Auditory secretaries thrive on being conversationally directed. Even if they are very bright, they'll understand what you want much better if you simply tell them.

The worst thing you can do is drop a bunch of paperwork

on his desk and set your hopes on having the work accurately completed and on time. Whatever these secretaries are given to do, they process instructions internally until it makes *auditory* sense to them. Only then will they proceed to accurately complete a task. So if you give them a bunch of visual instructions, you're handicapping them and your office time. Always give them a task verbally. If you absolutely must hand them visual information, make sure you stick around long enough to answer any questions they might have. The upside of all this is that once you fulfill their program for instructions, they are incredibly effective.

Auditory secretaries are very well spoken and are excellent liaisons on the phone. They understand language better than the other types and are predisposed to understanding dialects, regionalisms, and even subtongues. They won't have a problem with foreign languages, either. Auditories have an instinctive ability for extracting the meaning out of any language. I'm not saying that they can translate languages they haven't learned, just that they have a feeling for understanding what someone is saying, even when the verbal portion of the communication is coded differently.

Auditory secretaries are efficient in ways that are not as immediately apparent as, say, with visuals. They have a gestalt sense of order. They depend on hearing the entire scenario, rather than parts of it. That's why it's always better to involve your auditory secretary in what you're doing rather than giving her limited access to a particular project. And this is where the auditory's incredible sense of intuition becomes indispensable.

By all means, bring your auditory secretary into meetings with you. It'll be like having a stenographer present. Moreover, the auditory secretary will hear things you won't. Things like truthfulness, ambiguity, deceit, authenticity. Oftentimes he'll be able to give you terrific insight on how people are perceiving you. These secretaries make wonderful coaches and loyal supporters. Take advantage of their ability to decipher hidden agendas and double entendre. With an auditory secretary, you'll have the advantage of second sight, and you'll be able to get an edge on your adversaries. If you overlook her natural talents, you'll be depriving yourself.

Auditory secretaries will do excellent work if you are willing to listen openly to them. They will need verbal feedback and patience. If you're looking for a paper pusher, this is the wrong person for the job. But if you want an ally, oftentimes a shrewd one, listen to her as she speaks her mind. You'll be hearing pearls of wisdom.

5

KINESTHETIC OR FEELING-BASED EXECUTIVES AND BUSINESSPEOPLE

One of the most interesting relationships ever to have enraptured television viewing audiences was that of William Shatner's Captain Kirk and Leonard Nimoy's Spock. For more than twenty years, the friendship they shared while maintaining the roles of captain and first officer has enchanted all of us. For in these two were the living representations of the complexity of feelings and the sterile grace of their lack. Yet our unending interest is an odd one. For in this dynamic, we see a part of ourselves that frightens us. A part we may even dread. Deep down inside us, there is a collective symbolism that is born of complex fantasies. These fantasies engage us to pose the question: What would I be like if I didn't have feelings?

We all do have feelings; even the most despicable and unsavory of creatures relies on a sense of feeling. But kinesthetics are the representational type that relies most heavily on their *feelings* of experience. Although they have all the other senses that we collectively share, their perception of life is heavily biased by how they feel about their reality. To a kinesthetic's way of thinking, something has to feel a certain way before it can be considered acceptable. I'm sure you can see how this quality will direct these people in business.

Making up approximately 25 percent of the population,

kinesthetics are wonderful counselors, and they have a slant on things that most others do not. When a situation is being analyzed, the kinesthetic will always have another way of interpreting the facts. This is often based on his feelings. Now, one would be tempted to think how unreliable this is, especially in light of the economic climate of our time. But kinesthetics are brilliant businesspeople. If anything, they are the ones to be aware of, especially in the area of negotiation skills.

When I first began studying kinesthetics, I assumed that their heightened awareness of feelings would get in their way. And sometimes this is true. An undisciplined kinesthetic is someone who is out of control because he's at the mercy of his feelings. Lost in some short-circuited loop of conflicting emotions, he can be anything from sad and upset to a tyrant of the first order. But on the other side, a well-disciplined kinesthetic is a model of tempered authority, often the most respected member of the business community. And because of his intimate connection with his feelings, he can be extremely sensitive to others' feelings. All in all, a disciplined kinesthetic makes a terrific businessperson.

There are two kinds of kinesthetics. Or I should say there are two ways a kinesthetic will operate.

First, there is the internal kinesthetic. These people measure most of their experience by how they feel internally. Whether they are executives, or managers, or secretaries, or clients, they base a large portion of their perception on how people and places make them feel internally. They are truly feeling-based.

Then there are externally oriented kinesthetics. Because of their predisposition to *touch,* they tend to be hands-on in anything they do. They like to touch and will want to feel a product as part of their buying criteria. They tend also to physically touch others as they communicate. It's not that they're being overly familiar with people—although in a very personal sense they are—it's simply that they need to feel the object of their attention. If that happens to be a sweater, that's not a problem. But these people can sometimes get into trouble by the misinterpretation of their behavior—an unfortunate obstacle they consistently bump up against.

Of course, all of us—visuals, auditories, and kinesthetics—have a blend of internal and external kinesthetic properties. So the distinction I've made between these two subtypes is strictly as a further means of recognition. And you will use these subtle distinctions as you become more competent and fluid at influencing people.

For example:

Recently I went to lunch with a client who was considering using my services for his management consulting firm. They had serious problems in their negotiation skills, and sales had been way off for the last two quarters. If this client didn't do something quickly to turn his company around, he wouldn't have any company at all. I knew I had the answer for him—he couldn't afford not to hire me. But he was scared. And he had some people whispering to him that the answer lies in switching accounting practices.

We had lunch at the Four Seasons in New York City. Because it was such a beautiful day, we decided to walk our way back to the Plaza Hotel, where he was staying. As we walked up Fifth Avenue, we passed FAO Schwarz, the most incredible toy store in the world. He had never been there before and wanted to take a look inside. Well, instead of walking through, we ended up spending an hour looking at everything. My client was in pig heaven! Every time we came to another display, he would go right inside and get completely wrapped up in his feelings. His breathing would change; his eye accessing cues would shift lower right; and his language was really high touch. When he saw the Lionel electric trains, he had a grin on his face that was pure ecstasy.

As a chugging locomotive whizzed by and he whipped out his American Express card to pay for an antique train, I placed my hand on his elbow, went "Mmmmmm," as if I too were in absolute rapture (I was), and told him, "You made a great choice in coming here today. I'm glad you were able to do this for yourself."

What I did was take advantage of the wonderful state he was in by installing a reminder (the touch, the sound, and the statement), which I would be able to trigger off later when I wanted to have it available for another use. Like when he was deciding whether to hire me or not.

We met at his hotel suite for a final discussion. At one point we both got up for some freshly brewed coffee that room service had just delivered. As we stood side by side filling our cups, the aroma from the steaming brew made us both feel good. As he poured the coffee, I touched his elbow, inhaled more of the delicious aroma, and said, "Mmmmm." I followed that with, "Why don't we close a deal now?"

Do I really have to tell you I got the account? Let's just say that when I left that meeting, I, too, had a wide smile across my face. My understanding and utilization of NLP allowed me to accomplish my goal.

The point of all this is, of course, that noticing the fine distinctions of his kinesthetic personality allowed me to close a business deal in about a tenth the time and with hardly any undue angst. I had just to open my eyes and notice the way he sorted his experience. Did he make visual pictures like a visual? No, he never used visual language; he never looked up and to the left; he didn't use his body with visual dexterity. Did he have a dialogue within himself? I did notice some auditory activity going on inside. The train whistle almost blew him away, and he was subvocalizing some of the background music coming from the display speakers. But that notwithstanding, he was primarily a kinesthetic and represented his experience of reality through his kinesthetic representational system.

Because kinesthetics process thought by feelings, they tend to breathe quite deeply and oftentimes very slowly. If you've had the occasion to talk with someone at the office who seems very intent and patient with you while you talk, chances are you're watching a kinesthetic in action.

It is important to know that kinesthetics will experience and re-create in *their* experience whatever it is you're communicating to them. So you must be very responsible about how you talk with them. Especially in *context.* If you're telling them a specific business strategy, for example, they'll not only derive the meaning of the strategy, but your intention, motivation, and bias behind using it. Now, I'm not saying that kinesthetics are mind readers. I'm not saying that they jump to conclusions. I *am* saying that more than other representational types, kinesthetics will get the flavor of the whole stew. Though they're not auditory and won't key into voice tone or inflection, and though they're not visual and won't create a mental image of your meaning, they *will* get whatever spin you've managed to place on your subject matter—intentional or unintentional. So be forewarned. Of course, you will be able to use this to your advantage when you're selling or motivating or negotiating, because this knowledge, combined with other NLP skills, will enable you to really control the situation. For further information, see the chapter on strategies.

In general, kinesthetics speak in lower voices than others. I think this is one of their most obvious physical traits. They also tend to speak a little slower. This has to do with their need to run incoming and outgoing data through their feelings before speaking their thoughts. Which again points to the fact that just about everything these people do has to make sense to them on the level of feelings. If you extrapolate this to their business life, you will see how important it is to approach them in the right context.

Their bodies tend to be hard—especially if they are externally oriented kinesthetics. This comes from the fact that since they genuinely like touching, they gravitate to occupations where their sense of touch is utilized. This will also draw them to sports and physical activity. As a result, kinesthetics generally tend to be in better physical shape than the rest of us.

THE KINESTHETIC BOSS

One should never think that because kinesthetics are not visual or auditory, they can be easily manipulated. They cannot. Kinesthetics have such an incredible sense of feeling they'll often be one step ahead of you. They'll "sense" if something is good or bad for the company. And they'll get that sense much sooner than most of their advisors. Perhaps this is what makes kinesthetics so difficult to deal with at times. They will often run against the flow of opinion and do what they feel is best. This will drive auditory and visual managers crazy. But no matter how challenging, you must be able to achieve rapport with these people on *their* wavelength, not yours. That's the key to influencing kinesthetic bosses.

The kinesthetic boss, if he's a well-developed manager, will surround himself with people who communicate with him through feelings. He will also be available to look at what you show him and listen to what you have to say because he knows it's important to have these resources available to him. He will always prefer, however, to respond and gravitate to the feeling part of any input.

With kinesthetics, more than with any other representational type, mood swings will be a large factor in their behavior. You will have to watch closely for this and understand that it's okay to cancel an important meeting with them if it's not a good day. You're much better off having them upset with you for a broken agreement than to try to match wits with them when they are looping through an upset of their own. They just won't get off it as quickly as an auditory or a visual.

Kinesthetic bosses can be very seductive. They can lead you down the primrose path with unspoken promises. Therefore, they may lead you on with inferences they don't feel bound to honor. You must be on guard for this. If you feel there is an implied agreement between you, always try to get some sort of clarification. Kinesthetic bosses don't mind being questioned; they do mind being taken the wrong way.

If you want something from him or her, always frame your request in terms of feelings, whether internal or external. For instance, if you're interested in a promotion, whatever you do, don't try to impress your boss with looking the part. He couldn't be less interested. And I don't have to tell you by now that long-winded discourses on how much you've done and how much you deserve are a complete waste of breath. However, if you appeal to him on the level of feelings, you'll have a better than good chance.

How do you do this? Well, if you really want to influence him in a way that gets him to take action, you'll have to learn about strategies and anchoring. And if you care to get him thinking along the right lines, you'll have to have a working knowledge of eye accessing cues and mirroring, as well as language processing. You'll be learning these skills in the next chapters. But for now, you can try to relate to him or her with language-based thought. Create a feeling within him about you or your work through what you say. Do anything that provokes a feeling state. But be careful that you install the *right* feeling state. This can be tricky, so tread lightly. Because we haven't yet touched on exactly how this is done, it may not be the wisest move to attempt right now. Wait at least until we've covered mirroring and representational language—unless you feel like living dangerously. When you learn about strategies, you won't believe how powerful you'll be at manipulating the environment you share with your boss.

One last comment about the kinesthetic boss: Everything will impart a feeling in her. So take that into account when relating to her. Remember, too, humor is something that kinesthetics will think about way after you've left the office. They will get a definite feeling not only about the humorous interaction you've shared, but also about the subtle shadings that are implied in your humor. Of all the representational types, they are the most influenced by metaphor. They will loop through their feeling states over and over until arriving at a concrete sense of meaning. The bad part to this is that the state they arrive at may not be the one you want. So extra, extra care must be given to these types, especially if they are your boss.

THE KINESTHETIC SECRETARY

She'll really go the distance for you. But you must be sure to appeal to her through her sense of feeling. You must also observe the way she communicates with your clients, because kinesthetic secretaries have a tendency to get caught up in the *emotional* context of business. This can work for you or against you. If you employ an externally oriented kinesthetic, you'll get just the right amount of feeling or touch with the discharge of her responsibilities. You'll find that most everyone is delighted with her, that she's intuitive and innovative, and perhaps you'll discover how truly irreplaceable she is. On the other hand, if she's an internally oriented kinesthetic, you might have a problem because the majority of her experience is conveyed to her through a hierarchy of feeling states. The internally oriented kinesthetic secretary will become emotionally involved in many of her responsibilities. Havoc may ensue. This is quite common and can be extremely frustrating. When your secretary has very strong feelings that are generated toward someone you're doing business with, it can complicate the entire process. For instance, if she likes the other party, will she make it easier for that person to gain access to you? Will she try to sway you in one direction or another out of feelings instead of prudent business judgment? And if she dislikes the other party, how will that affect this person's ability to talk with you? Will she unconsciously sabotage or miscommunicate a delicate point? In a large proportion of the cases I've worked with, the internal kinesthetic can, and will, get caught up with unnecessary emotional excess, which oftentimes damages the executive-client relationship.

I'm friends with a man who is the founding partner of an extraordinarily successful television syndication company. He's a terrific person. Unpretentious, committed to his work, and even-tempered. People are genuinely attracted to him, and he's known within his industry to be a just and honorable man.

But his secretary is a problem. She's an internally oriented kinesthetic who cannot leave her feelings about business at home. She is alternately good and bad to callers, depending on how she feels about them. In a very strong sense, her attitudes can determine the course of her boss's company. And so through her, my friend gets a deeply personalized view of nearly everyone he does business with. At the beginning he thought she was a terrific asset, because she gave him a lot of insight to people with whom he did business. But as time went on, the emotional baggage his secretary weighed in with began to take its toll. Complaints, miscommunication, altercations between secretary and vendor—it became a mess. For the longest time, no one knew what to do. Then, finally, after much too long a time, the secretary was discharged. Only much later on did my friend find out that everyone knew his business because his secretary had feelings about everything he did. And shared them with everyone. She did this not because she's a bad person, but because she'd loop through her feelings internally, creating an unproductive vacillation of attitudes that never served anyone and needed people to unload on in order to stay on an even keel.

This woman was an extreme case. But her story highlights the importance both of knowing what representational type of individual is working for your company, and using good screening procedures with *all* employee placements. This way you'll avoid an obstacle that many have bumped up against.

Because of her sensitivity, the kinesthetic secretary will likely be involved with you, your clients, subordinates, and staff. This may work to your advantage. It can provide you with an excellent source of public relations. Be sensitive to her needs and she'll give you a hundred and ten percent. She'll make a good confidante. She'll understand whatever your problems are—even the ones she has difficulty relating to. And oftentimes, she'll have wonderful counsel to offer. Take advantage of this. Actually, it's not really taking advantage because interacting with her on the level of feelings is what makes sense to her. It's an altogether safe place from which she can communicate.

The kinesthetic secretary will also *sort* by feelings. That means she'll code information about business by prioritizing it according to how she feels about it, or according to how she feels *you'll* feel about it. So most of the work she does will fit into some behavioral projection. The most obvious example of this is the way she'll set up your appointments. Your day will be planned out by what she senses are your high and low periods. You can readily see how important it is, then, that you let her know if her appraisal of your feeling states is accurate or not. Once she makes the needed course corrections, she'll provide you with incredibly smooth sailing. Don't be put off by her attempts to gain insight into your moods and states. This is just her way of putting the responsibilities of her job in some sort of feeling-based perspective.

THE KINESTHETIC CLIENT

Selling the kinesthetic client, negotiating with him, and relating to him *must* be done on the level of feelings. More than with any other of the representational types, the kinesthetic client or customer will be extremely receptive to you if you speak to him with your feelings. That means whatever it is you're selling—be it a product or service—your chances of closing will largely depend on your ability to frame your sale within the parameters of feelings.

The kinesthetic client always needs to get a feeling about what you're saying. You'll notice this client will keep asking you the same questions in different ways until you satisfy his feeling-based criteria. Some people mistake this for stupidity, but this is not the case. In fact, kinesthetic clients will often be remarkably insightful. They will read you like a crystal ball. They have a built in fail-safe system that warns them when someone is speaking less than truthfully. The probability of buyer's remorse is greater with this representational type than with any other. If you succeed in selling them a bill of goods, you may expect them to return it rather quickly—if they didn't really want it in the first place.

Visual buyers—and, to a large extent, auditory buyers—will not have the patience level you'll find in a kinesthetic. The kinesthetic will give you the opportunity to sell over and over again. But kinesthetics won't buy if you don't make them feel a certain way about you, or your service, or your product. Continually showing them demonstrations, or repeating the benefits of your wares, will tire them. They want to feel one way or the other.

Earlier on in my career, I gave a beautiful presentation to the vice president of an insurance company. It was the most articulate and visually appealing pitch I had ever made, and I was sure I had the deal. But in my enthusiasm I forgot that she was a pure kinesthetic, and though she was courteous enough to feign interest, I had gotten nowhere. Looking somewhat pained, she said:

"Well, what's your gut reaction? Do you think you can help us?"

It was only at that moment that I realized I had been selling her incorrectly. This woman didn't care about my storyboards or charts; she didn't savor my eloquence; she wanted to *feel* one way or another about what I was selling her. So I sat down and told her how she'd feel after I redesigned their sales training program. I told her that she'd have a real sense of accomplishment and satisfaction after the training. I brightened up and put on a smile instead of looking so somber. And I asked her to remember a time when she pulled off a real sales training coup. When she started to associate to those feelings, I raised my voice with excitement and said:

"That's what I'm going to do. I'm going to bring back that sense of effectiveness to your selling approach. This department will have a whole new life to it. People will sell more effectively because they will be excited about the product they're selling!"

I had gotten through. She had an immediate state shift. You could see it. She sat up, looked interested, crossed her legs into a relaxed position, and even cracked a smile.

"Okay. I'll try it. Let's run with it and hope it works."

The very fact that kinesthetics give you their time usually indicates that they have already begun to react kinesthetically to you or your product. But it's up to you to close by framing your sales presentation within their domain of feelings.

Causing a kinesthetic to react is simple. You just add emotion to whatever it is you're communicating. You may do this in a number of ways. You may convey whatever feeling you deem appropriate to the presentation either by demonstrating it in yourself or by installing it in your buyer. For a further discussion of exactly how this is done, see the chapter on strategies and state induction.

If possible, let kinesthetic clients physically touch your product. If it's a service, then let them feel the brochure or prospectus. Always try to satiate their sense of feelings. This holds true whether they are externally or internally oriented. Even the most internally oriented kinesthetic will be excited by feeling a physical part of your sale. If you don't do this, you are cutting down your chances of closing.

If you sell in a showroom and don't actively encourage your kinesthetic patrons to get their hands on your product, you're automatically missing out on a higher percentage of income. Nine out of ten kinesthetics will ultimately take a pass on your product if you don't allow them to get their hands dirty—even if they initially responded to it. That's because what they see is only a small part of their internal experience. Most of them will pass you right by if left strictly to their eyes and ears. I can't emphasize this enough. You must be able to code your communication so that kinesthetically oriented people will totally understand you. It's that simple.

Kinesthetics are so plugged in to coding their experience in terms of feelings that even emotion that is opposite to what you really want will produce a sort of challenging interest. In the previous example, the fact that I got the vice president of sales to respond was an accomplishment in itself. With kinesthetics, you can work your way from emotion to emotion, even if you start with a negative emotion. Getting them to feel is the key. It can give you a springboard off of which to work.

<< >>

The kinesthetic boss, secretary, and customer all share one common denominator: They relate to the world through the way the world makes them feel. If what's outside makes them feel good, then they'll plunge in, full steam ahead, fully engaged, in total participation. However, if they can't get a grasp on what's being presented to them, if they can't make sense out of the stimuli they're being asked to choose from, and if feelings aren't a dominant part of your presentation, then they'll withdraw. They'll be very nice about it, but your vote will be canceled. When you interact with these people, let your heart show you the way. You'll be surprised at how far you'll get.

6

WINNING BY REFLECTION—THE MIRRORING AND PACING OF POWER

At the very heart of NeuroLinguistic Programming is the fundamental ability to align oneself with another in such a powerful way that our very behavior is irresistibly persuasive. This is achieved with many levels of technology, starting with the most simple and conscious and progressing on to the deeply complex and subconscious. However, none of these resourceful states is complicated in the sense of being difficult to learn. In fact, many of them will come to you very naturally. Indeed, you are using some of them already. The secret in learning NLP is not in the discovery of some mystical secret, but in being conscious of what we already do that works.

The most basic level of influence in NLP is **mirroring**. Mirroring is nothing more than behavior that offers back to its observers a reflection of themselves. But it has an almost magical power because of the way people respond to their own behavior. They *relate* to it and perceive it with great affinity. It is the most comfortable and reassuring phenomenon that happens outside of themselves. This reaction has its genesis in the symbiotic and deeply archetypical relationship we have with our parents while infants. Nothing in life ever so completely satisfies us as the expression of ourselves in others which we so rarely perceive. It is therefore a powerful tool we can work with when attempting to bring others into rapport with us. In fact, if you look up the definition of *rapport*, you'll find it is a state achieved by offering back to others *their* behavior with grace and elegance.

Mirroring others is something we've continually done since the very beginning of our lives. Students of behavior and language acquisition know that mirroring occurs right after the period of babbling and just before the stage of echolalia. We unconsciously mirror others because it's very comfortable for us to do so. It's also a very basic survival mechanism.

Something within directs us to mirror others so that we can get along with them better. From our earliest months of training, we are constantly taught the value of being able to get along with others. We "imitate" what others are doing—first to impress them and show them how able we are, and then, later, to try to be more like them. Researchers from Freud to Piaget to Harry Stack Sullivan have acknowledged the mirroring process. The late Virginia Satir even categorized different negotiating types based almost exclusively on mirroring. And, of course, Bandler and Grinder expanded on this phenomenon in their brilliant early works on NeuroLinguistic Programming itself.

In adulthood, we call those who outshine us in this ability charismatic.

People who are charismatic are able to make us like them even if we start out biased against them. Something in them is so appealing we oftentimes are willing to go out of our way to please them. We do this because it brings us pleasure.

Why?

Because, in these people, we see ourselves.

Charisma is nothing more than the ability to conform ourselves to others to such a degree that others experience us as though we were a reflection of themselves. Let me give you that again:

> **CHARISMA IS THE ABILITY TO CONFORM OURSELVES TO OTHERS SO THAT OTHERS EXPERIENCE US AS A REFLECTION OF THEMSELVES.**

Contrary to popular belief, there is no magic chemistry in acquiring charisma. It's simply a matter of learning its behavioral technology. We all want to maximize our potential so that we can pull ahead of the crowd and do things that will enable us to reap the rewards to which we feel we're entitled. What mirroring is about is beginning that process whereby we bring others—visuals, auditories, and kinesthetics—into rapport with us, and hence, under our control.

Most of us think that being different is the way to make it in this world. We've always heard that opposites attract. Well, they don't. Although from time to time we find our opposites very appealing—even exciting—really, how long does this usually last? Think back to the last time you sustained a healthy and profitable business relationship with someone who was the opposite of you—someone who thought differently, spoke differently, liked different things, was happy about things that made you sad. Now tell me: Are you really comfortable with him or her? Do you go out of your way to do business with this person? Or do you consistently go back to the person you feel comfortable with? You know, that supplier who has the same laugh or finds the same things funny that you do. Or that manager who adores skiing the way you do.

If you're the president of your company, who will you advance: the VP who reminds you of you years ago, or that other guy who's real competent but who relates to people exactly the opposite the way you do? If you're a secretary, to whom do you feel more responsive: the guy you're able to identify with, or someone else who's just as nice but whose personality is alien to you?

Let me ask you this: When you get your hair cut, do you switch haircutters each time? Of course not. Do you know why? I'll bet you think it's because your haircutter gives you the best cut around. But if you really look at it closely, and you're very honest with yourself, you'll discover that your hair pretty much looks the same now as it did four haircutters ago. The difference is that with your current haircutter you feel the most comfortable. That's the truth. Studies prove this! There's something about your current haircutter that makes you feel good. He makes you feel as though you're okay. And if you think about it, you'll realize that he reminds you a little of yourself—at least in some ways. They may be subtle ways, like the sound of his voice, or his posture, or his views about people; maybe it's his attitude, or his sense of humor. In any event, I'll bet he's more like you than the others preceding him. You see, in not so few ways, you and your haircutter are in rapport.

When you're in rapport with another, your chances of getting what you want are magnified significantly. This is so because there are *two* of you rooting for you. Your concerns are his concerns; and his concerns are yours. It's natural, and it's something that can be maximized to the point where each of you can influence the other to the degree whereby you each achieve a deep rapport.

<< >>

Can you recall mirroring someone today? Because you did, you know. If you want to see this happening right before your eyes, try a little experiment. Tomorrow, when you go in to the office, I want you to notice how you feel with the different people you interact with. Take an emotional inventory with each person. When you find someone with whom you're really communicating well, notice how each of you is physically situated. If you're sitting, are you both in the same position, or at least in similar positions? Are your arms in the same position as the other person's? Are you both smiling or nodding, or are your heads in the same tilt or incline? If you're standing, notice if both of you are in similar positions. Notice if there's any similarity to what both of you are physically doing.

Most likely, you'll find that there *is* a similarity. Some of you will be shocked when you realize how close you come to modeling what the other person is doing. I suggest to you that the more rapport you're in with the person to whom you're communicating, the more you'll be mirroring each other. And as this process continues and builds, the deeper the rapport becomes.

Did you know at that moment in time—at that very moment when you're in perfect alignment with that other person—you can influence and persuade him to do whatever it is you want him to do? In truth, if you knew what you'll know by the end of this book, you'd be able to accomplish virtual miracles of business finesse. You'd be able to get what you want easier and with less aggravation. You'd be able to do it in one quarter of your usual time, and you'd be that much more satisfied with yourself after accomplishing it.

Mirroring is the vanguard of this process.

MIRRORING

Mirroring takes place on many logical levels and within a multitude of contexts. But suffice to say that mirroring begins on the grossest level. In mirroring, we enter the realm of both the macro and the micro—although not necessarily in that order. You'll find that sometimes the grossest level of mirroring—say, body positon—will effect the behavioral change you want. On other occasions, it may take finer distinctions of mirroring to accomplish a particular outcome.

When you go to a ball game, take a look down the aisle in which you're sitting. You'll see a majority of the people are sitting just like you are. They will probably have similar expressions on their faces. They'll be eating and drinking at the same rate as you, too. Even their breathing patterns are in synch with yours. If you doubt this, look around you the next time a heavy-duty play is taking place. Everybody will be in rapport. In fact the rapport will be so high that strangers will talk to you—and you to them—without even being introduced. You've probably never even thought about it, but you could close the deal of the year right in the middle of a ball game.

I did.

Recently I was invited to a basketball game in New York City by the top man responsible for secondary public education in a western state. He was in New York to interview a few consultants in my field. I really wasn't too thrilled about the invitation. I'm not a basketball fan, and I was even less a fan of this particular person. He was pleasant and gracious enough to me, but I just couldn't take to him. There wasn't terribly good chemistry going on either side, I'm afraid. But I'll tell you, I wanted this deal. I wanted it because, for me, it represented the possibility of actually making a contribution to society. And I wasn't going to let my feelings about this guy, or anything else, stand in my way.

Well, this normally reserved, authoritative-looking guy went nuts during the game. When his team scored, look out. He was up in his seat—if not standing on it—yelling at the top of his lungs. And he swore like sailor. I'd never before heard some of the expressions he used. It was unbelievable. And the more he carried on, the crazier I got.

He had an annoying habit of suddenly surprising me

with very specific business conversation right after he'd go bananas over an exciting play. Each time this happened, he'd go wild—totally distracting me from the game and our business conversation—then would quickly regain his composure, settle back down in his seat, and take up the conversation from precisely where he'd left off. And he'd remember exactly what the hell he said, as though nothing had happened. It was unnerving. Until I remembered mirroring.

I must tell you, even I get tired of using NLP all the time. Sometimes I just want to be completely off purpose. But the goal that night was to get the job done. I wanted what this guy had to offer. I just didn't expect an opportunity to grasp it right at that specific moment. But I did. I mirrored him. I got into the game. I started yelling and shouting. I began to talk with everyone around me. And even though I felt weird doing that, everyone around me thought I was totally natural. I mirrored everything he did, being careful not to mimic and to be respectful. I gave myself permission to let go and climb to a different level. But a specific level: his level. And then an odd thing happened: I really started to enjoy the game. I really did. I totally stepped into the experience. I ended up having a great time. And so did he. And I got the work.

Now, I'm not trying to be simplistic or patronizing. I'm not saying that all you have to do is mirror someone and everything will work out. But oftentimes it will! And even if it doesn't happen for you right there, it's important to begin the process of rapport with mirroring.

Another thing to keep in mind is that the example I just gave is a dramatic case. Most of your theater will be at the office. And you must remember to start out easy. NLP is very powerful and must be used with great care—especially at the beginning. But let me also say this: You *will* reach a point in your sophistication where nothing will be impossible! And your training will be a hundred percent faster than mine because I didn't have an NLP business book to learn from.

Mirroring is something you'll want to do with everyone

because it's practically effortless, and it produces terrific results. It doesn't require that you have anything at stake to have it work for you. You simply have to remember to use it to make things happen.

Whenever I go in to a business meeting, I always mirror whomever it is I'm talking with. From the moment the elevator doors open until I get back in my car, I'm mirroring. As I address each individual, I mirror their presentation.

The following are some of the general parameters of mirroring. Remember though, that *all* behavior can be mirrored. While it's good for you to learn the basics, I strongly encourage you to experiment with any parameters you feel confident about. Mirroring is one of those methods that lends itself very well to experimentation. When I do professional NLP trainings, I make sure that every participant discovers at least one new parameter of mirroring that he or she ordinarily would never think of using. Usually this very behavior is the one that becomes their favorite.

There is one caveat in mirroring, however. And I can't stress too much how important it is never to violate it: Never, never mimic.

NEVER MIMIC

In our society, there is a negative social taboo in mimicking. We have a very strong cultural restraint against it. Not only is it considered rude, but it will do nothing to cause rapport.

How do we mirror without mimicking? We assume the responses that are closest to direct mimicking. We also slow down our responses so that they trail the behavior of the other party. That's okay to do because the mind has a built-in delay mechanism of plus or minus seven chunks of information. This plus or minus seven chunks makes it possible to delay the presentation of material. So when someone stands a certain way, I'll take *almost* that position a few seconds after they do. When they move a hand, I'll also move my hand, but I'll do it a few seconds later. Moreover, I'll often mirror with opposites.

Mirroring with opposites is just that: You mirror by using opposite body parts. If someone takes their left hand and adjusts the knot in his tie, you can use your right hand to brush some lint off of your lapel or blouse. Remember, in mirroring you don't want to mimic. *Similar* behaviors are best. In fact, I'd say that similar movements are definitely the way to go.

Stance

Mirroring the way a person stands and carries herself is the first thing you'll want to do. You can start by noticing the way she's leaning; you can notice how her posture is aligned. Assume that posture and direction. You'll notice right away that people have a great assortment of standing positions. And these positions change as we communicate. Often our physical stance is strongly tied to the kinesthetic representations of our thoughts. But you needn't be concerned with that just now. It's good enough simply to mirror, or cross mirror those we want to influence.

Head Position

Try to angle your head in the same way that the other person does. Again, this should be done so that you *generally* conform to another. You want to avoid doing the *exact* same thing he is doing.

Voice

This might sound strange to you, but people like to hear similarity in vocal patterns as well as anything else. People feel more comfortable with someone who speaks the way they do. I know you think it's charming to hear a southern accent in a salesman, or a down-home western accent in a vice president or manager. And it is. For a while. Then, if their regionalism is *not* your natural inflection—take it from me—the mind automatically begins to consider this person alien. From another region of life.

I have a friend who sells his consulting services around the country at conventions. He's a terrific salesman and was well received everywhere, except in Alabama. No matter what he did, his sales statistics in that state were brutal. For a long time he didn't confide this to anyone. Then one day he asked for my help. I attended one of his seminars and found him to be pleasing enough; in retrospect, his style of speaking was rather good. He was a great storyteller, often referring to his father, a well-known jurist. But he failed miserably at gaining rapport in one particular part of the country. He failed to mirror not only the regional dialect, but the local ideology as well. I found out that in Alabama, his constant references to his father were actually insulting to the citizens of that state. You see, Alabamans refer to God as father. When they refer to their male parent they are more likely to use the expression *daddy*. So any rapport he might have had with these people was constantly being compromised by his lack of mirroring the local or regional dialect and ideology. When he began to mirror their very attractive drawl, and quit referring to his dad as father, his sales took off. It was that black and white. Mirroring is that simple and effective.

Other parameters of the voice that can be easily mirrored are:

Volume
Accents
Rhythm
Intonation
Cadence
Timbre
Tone

Breathing Patterns

This is my favorite. Mirroring someone's breathing pattern is so subtle and such a highly unconscious process that it always goes undetected and is therefore an excellent way of generating rapport. This is because breathing is directly and intimately linked to our emotional states. Don't you breathe differently when you're excited or bored? How about when you're frightened or passionate? Can you recall how you breathe when you're totally interested? To a very large degree, breathing controls our inner states. Notice the way your prospective client breathes and match it. People fall into a very strong rapport with those who breathe like themselves.

Kinesthetics usually breathe on the deeper side and with fuller respirations. When I'm talking with an obvious kinesthetic, that's the way I breathe. I'm not saying to do this to the point where you pass out (that would definitely break rapport), but I *am* saying to mirror the other person's breathing to the degree that it engenders rapport. This means, with kinesthetics, that an occasional deep breath and a sigh here and there will do the trick. The nifty part about doing this is, for me, how relaxed I get. In fact, I get so relaxed that everything else involved in the sale goes rather smoothly. This is in direct contrast to the breathing rapport one must find with a visual, whose breaths are short and shallow. This is quite uncomfortable for me, so I when I start feeling strange, I stop. Then a few minutes later I continue.

One of my best-kept secrets is the *manual* way I gain trust and rapport—and hence results—through pacing another's breathing. I simply use some part of myself to keep tempo with another's pattern of breathing. Try this yourself. The next time you're in a business meeting and want to influence someone, mirror and pace his breathing rhythm by tapping your finger in time to his respirations or breaths. I do this all the time because by now people watch me like a hawk. So I had to devise finer distinctions of mirroring. This one works particularly well.

Mirroring Statements

This kind of mirroring has a hypnotic effect. It dramatically opens people to suggestion. It works this way. When someone tells you a fact about herself, wait awhile, then give it back to her within the context of the sale. For instance, if someone has told you she prefers ninety-day CDs, but you're selling one-hundred-twenty-day CDs, you would feed her back her own truthful fact, but within your pace.

> "You've told me that you want to buy nineties, and they actually are a good short-term investment. Since I know all about these sorts of things, I'll show how much more money you'll make with one-twenties."

What you're doing is mirroring her statement, then pacing and leading her to your point of view. By pacing statements, you create an agreement frame through which you get the result you want, in addition to the rapport you need.

PACING AND LEADING

Pacing accomplishes two objectives, both of them quite important. First, it is the best way for you to actually test if, in fact, someone is in rapport with you. Second, pacing allows you to lead someone exactly where you want to take him. Used intelligently and ethically, the impact this will have in all your business dealings is enormous.

Assuming your mirroring technique is working, pacing and leading are two ways of testing to see if you are, in effect, generating enough power to have the outcome you desire. They provide a true and objective way for you to have an accurate perception of what's taking place "out there."

Pacing and leading are extraordinarily easy behaviors to master. Here's the way it's done: When you want to test for rapport, simply take the lead and see if your partner is following. That is, instead of following whatever the other person is doing, immediately shift into a leadership mode. Easily. Subtly. Then notice whether the other person is following *your* behavior. If someone is, in fact, in rapport with you, he or she will begin to mirror whatever it is you're doing.

I once chaired a think tank for psychologists called "Psychological Issues in Contemporary Neuroperception." As part of the course, and as a demonstration of the power of pacing and leading, I took ten of the brightest doctoral fellows with me on an interview to one of the nation's biggest long-distance phone companies. I wanted to demonstrate the effectiveness of pacing and leading. I had arranged permission to do this with the company's vice president of sales training, who, by the way, turned out to be very resistant. But nonetheless, I put on a great show.

The eleven of us walked into this man's office and completely filled all open sitting space. That immediately annoyed him. Then, when he began to realize that this was not just a business call, but a field trip—with him as the specimen in question—he truly broke rapport and became openly antagonistic and uncooperative. But before things got too out of hand, I began mirroring him. However, instead of taking two or three minutes, it took me well over ten minutes before I felt good enough to try a pace and lead. When I did, nothing happened. Back to more mirroring. This time, another ten minutes. Test for rapport again by taking the lead. Voilà. Success. To my relief—and to my fellow psychologists' amazement—this formerly resistant man, a walking objection, began to follow my behavior. When I crossed my legs, he followed. When I played with a paper clip, he fingered his fountain pen. When I shifted in my chair, so did he. It was a terrific demonstration of leading. But beyond the parlor magic, what did it really say? In his subconscious mind it said, "This guy's turned out to be just like me. I trust him now. He reminds me of myself. I've got to listen to what he has to say." And he did. In fact, I wasn't really looking for anything other than a field demo that day. However, we slipped into such a trusting state that I ended up speaking to his executive committee the very next week. From there, I instituted an NLP training program that is still running today.

Pacing is the process of mirroring and matching any observable behavior in your prospect. It allows you to present yourself in a way that generates deep levels of rapport. And remember, your presentation is *everything*. You see, people truly respond dramatically to *how* you present information. That's just a fact. If you represent yourself to someone as being like him or her, you're going to almost certainly make that sale. But the more unlike or dissimilar you are—

the more foreign you seem—the less likelihood you'll have of succeeding.

Through pacing, objections become an ally. It allows you to handle objections from your boss, prospective clients, committees—just about anyone—with an ease you've never encountered before. NLP allows you to take those objections and recode them to generate leverage with your subject.

Remember that mirroring is the foundation for all rapport. I suggest that you start to use mirroring right away. Practice it all the time. In a short while it will blend itself right into your natural presentation. When you apply mirroring at the office, you'll discover that others will like you more, that clients will be persuaded more easily, that the boss will be easier to get along with. And when you combine mirroring with the other techniques you'll master in this book, your business life will take on a beautiful new direction. Mirroring those you do business with reflects an irresistible rapport and creates winning results.

7

READING YOUR CLIENTS' AND COLLEAGUES' MINDS—WITH EYE ACCESSING CUES

Before we move on to the applied power portion of this book, I want to introduce you to a part of NeuroLinguistic Programming that is truly unique. The tool you're about to learn is an instrument through which you'll be able to read others' thoughts. Hard to believe? Yes, I know. I was one of its biggest skeptics when I first came across it, as well. But nevertheless, it works. The power of using **eye accessing cues** is one of the more useful cornerstones of this technology. I'm not a terribly great advocate of fortune-telling, but I predict that of all the skills you take away from this book, recognizing eye accessing cues will be the skill you use and remember the most. That's because it's the most revealing of other people's thoughts.

Eye accessing cues, like most of the somatic cues we consistently use, enable us to make better contact with a visual, auditory, or kinesthetic thought that has arisen into consciousness. Cues of these sort don't actually contribute to the communication we deliver, but they act as tiny catalysts in bringing that communication to completion. I believe that of all these cues, the eye accessing cue delivers the best and most accurate information to the informed observer.

Drs. Bandler and Grinder first discovered the phenomena in the early 1970s while researching various models of communication. Their work led them to study with Dr. Milton Erickson, generally thought of as the greatest medical hypnotherapist of his time. Originally, Bandler and Grinder were theorizing about the process of modeling, whereby one learns at a much-accelerated pace by coding information as closely as possible to someone who has perfected a specific behavior. That is to say, they were interested in modeling or "copying" positive and worthwhile behavior in others and seeing if, in fact, they could "install" that very same behavior in themselves or those they were treating. Somewhere along the way, they discovered that the way people move their eyes is directly correlated to the representational system they are thinking in. As time went on, these eye movement patterns proved to be astoundingly accurate indicators and have since become a cornerstone in the practice of NLP.

I think each of us knows, or remembers, someone whose eye movements can invariably be predicted. There are always some people who are unable to look directly into your eyes. For instance, one particular fellow I know would have great eye contact with me until he stopped talking and began listening. Then his eyes would almost always glance down to his lower right. This annoyed the hell out of me, and I assumed that he had so much internal noise in his life that he simply was unable to look me straight in the eye.

In the early 1970s, Werner Erhard conceived the *est* training. For many years *est* was thought of by many people to be the state of the art in dynamic seminar training. Interestingly, one of the basic tenets of the *est* philosophy was that people, in their ordinary day-to-day lives, were unable to "be" with other people because of a basic inability to directly experience others without having parallel thoughts and feelings. Werner and associates attributed this to the barriers we place between us and the outside world. That was the reason he gave for people not being able to look at other people in the eyes. A lot of people, including a lot of psychologists, agreed with this notion. I, too, was a great advocate of the *est* training. But *est* proved to be wrong. You see, people *have* to move their eyes to gain access to most representations. It's literally impossible to have certain classes of thought and not move your eyes. That blew the myth of great eye contact wide open.

It was determined by Bandler and Grinder that people use their eyes to stimulate different parts of their brain. The reason for this is that moving one's eyes in specified ways stimulates the brain to create a more accurate representation of cathected thought. That is to say, certain eye movements stimulate and produce certain classes of thoughts. Depending on which movement one uses, the brain will have an easier time of creating and making that particular thought more vivid and real. This isn't random movement. It is predictable and has a definite circumscribed path—depending on the *kind* of thought one is having at the moment.

Let me explain what each movement means, then draw a diagram as a graphic representation to assist you in recognizing them. After I've chartered out this new territory, we'll delve into the reason eye accessing cues are so fundamentally important for you to know, and how to use them to create a persuasive rapport.

EYE ACCESSING CUES

$-V^r-$

When we look up and to the left, we're accessing a *visual remembered* image. This means that whatever we're thinking about at that moment is taking the configuration of an image or picture from the past. That could mean our past of five minutes or forty years ago. For our purposes, time sequence is not important. What is relevant is that whether we are responding to a question that's been put to us, or simply off in our own world thinking, when we look up and to the left we're engaged in the process of visual thought that took place somewhere in the past. We call this position the visual remembered position, and designate it as V^r.

$—V^c—$

When we look up and to our right, we're accessing a *visual constructed* image. That's a visual picture of someone or something that hasn't taken place yet. It may be in the future, or it may simply be something we're trying to imagine. In either case the image is constructed, and one that we fabricate for ourselves at the moment. We refer to this eye accessing cue as the visual constructed cue and designate it as V^c.

$—A^r—$

When we look to our level left, we're accessing an *auditory remembered* thought. That means we're thinking about something that is expressing its meaning as an auditory representation. This could mean the sound of someone's voice, the sound of a client's office, the sound of a computer—any auditory sound that's from the past. When we look level left, we're processing experience with an auditory presentation. We refer to this as the auditory remembered position and designate it as A^r.

$—A^c—$

As the visual constructed eye access cue is to the visual remembered cue, so the *auditory constructed* eye accessing cue is to the auditory remembered cue. When we look to the level right, we're thinking in a constructed auditory perception. That is to say, that when we notice people glancing to their level right, they're trying to construct or imagine the sound of something they haven't heard before. It might be the sound of someone's voice, the way they would like to sound at next week's board meeting, or it may be their new secretary's voice. We refer to this as an auditory construction and designate it as A^c.

$—A^i—$

The auditory representational system has the distinction of possessing a *third* eye accessing cue. When we have an *auditory internal dialogue*—that is, an internal conversation with ourselves—we glance to our lower left. You'll notice this when someone you know is comparing two sides of a story. In sales, this is apparent when a prospective client is shopping for the best buy or product. This eye accessing cue is designated by the symbol A^i.

$—K—$

The last eye accessing cue is the one that represents our feeling state. It has only one position. When we step into our sense of emotion, we usually glance to our *lower right*. The designation for this is **K**. The *K* stands for *kinesthetic,* which is Latin for feelings.

<<>>

THERE ARE TWO BEHAVIORAL CONSIDERATIONS FOR EYE ACCESSING CUES:

1. The right and left movements of eye accessing cues are for right-handed people only. **Lefties reverse directions.** That is, visual remembered is upper right; visual constructed is upper left; auditory remembered is level right; auditory constructed is level left; internal dialogue is lower right; and kinesthetic is lower left. Approximately 10 percent of the population will have their eye accessing cues reversed. Just enough to keep you on your toes.

2. You've got to remember that when someone is facing you and looking, let's say, upper left, it's going to look to you as upper right. Keep in mind that eye accessing cue directions are descriptions of how *others* use them—not how you see them. Don't forget this. Remember that what's lower right to another is going to appear as lower left to you.

On the following pages are the graphic representations of eye accessing cues. Study them. Practice identifying them when you're talking with others. At first you'll find that you may have to pay close attention. However, after a brief time they'll become second nature to you.

So that you may study eye accessing cues individually, you will find each position diagramed separately with its description and designation on the following pages.

At this point you may be asking yourself, "Now that I know about eye accessing cues, what exactly will they do for me in terms of influencing and persuading others?" Good question.

Eye accessing cues will allow you to read people in a way you've never thought possible. They will permit you to know what someone is thinking about when you're doing business with that person—if not necessarily in content, then certainly in context. When you observe another looking up and to *his* left, you'll know he is accessing a visual remembered image. That means that he is seeing a picture of what you're communicating. If you ask someone what kind of computer she's in the market for and she looks upper left, you'll know she is seeing a picture of exactly what she wants. If you have this kind of information, you're going to be able to offer your customer exactly what she wants, and you'll be able to close much more effectively. You'll know how to relate to her because you'll know how she's thinking.

Eye Accessing Cues

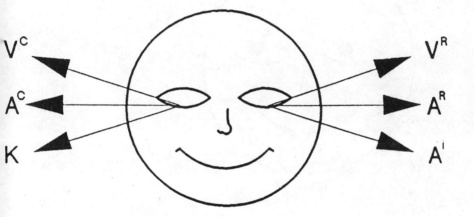

Visual Remembered Images

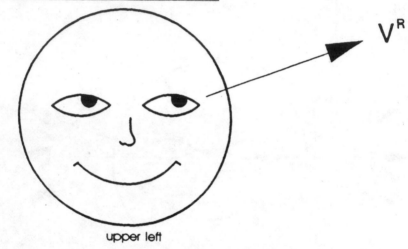

upper left

Visual Constructed Images

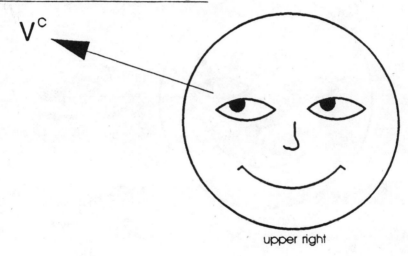

upper right

Auditory Remembered

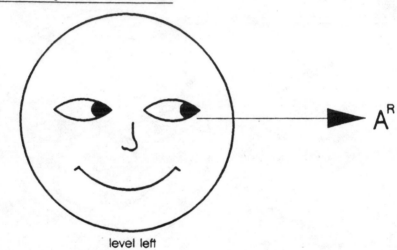

level left

Auditory Constructed

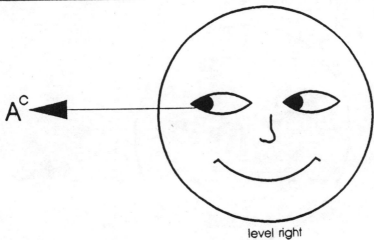

level right

Auditory Dialogue

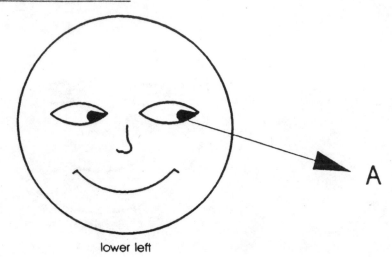

lower left

Kinesthetic

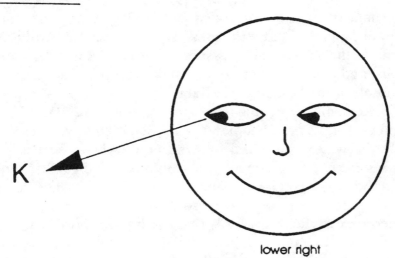

lower right

If a customer expresses her needs auditorily, then you'll frame your suggestions auditorily. If you can read your boss's eye accessing cues and ascertain he's promoting people who demonstrate kinesthetic attributes for a particular position, for starters you'll be able to use language that will appeal to him kinesthetically. If your colleague is using his visual eye accessing cues while asking you about a new project, you'll respond to him visually, possibly by showing him what you can do via a report or demonstration. In other words, when people exhibit specific eye accessing cues while communicating with you, you'll be able to answer their questions or challenges or statements not only with the appropriate data, but framed and coded with *their* specific representational language and strategies. This will automatically put you on their wavelength, dispense with any misunderstandings, and position you to really make yourself understood—and all in the best possible light.

Remember: **People like people who are like themselves.** People *trust* people who are like themselves. It's simply the way we're wired up. Therefore when you use eye accessing cues to augment your communication skills, you'll also be turning on higher levels of rapport. In essence, to the unconscious part of the person your talking with, you'll become very familiar. And trustworthy. On more than one level, you'll be mirroring so effectively that your powers of influence and persuasion will be super enhanced.

Now, am I talking about giving up who you are? No. Am I encouraging you to give up your personality and be a chameleon with others? Not at all. I *am* saying that others will relate to you and be on the same wavelength as you, and that they'll fall into a deep *rapport* with you, if you're able to *appear* to them as though you're like them. For how long? For as long as it takes. In many instances, that might mean a minute or two. Sometimes it could mean five minutes, or ten minutes. I've even had the occasion where I had to zap someone for twenty minutes. But that didn't mean I had to give up my ethical standards, or my integrity, or any part of me as an individual. It simply means that *for that specified amount of time* I had to be *flexible* enough so as to generate enough power that I could accomplish my goal. If you use this technology, you will have that result.

Now let's talk for a moment about context.

Eye accessing cues will be your magic wand on the road to power. They are the map that you'll use to check on your journey. Sometimes they'll be like radar or sonar, in that you'll depend on them as if you're traveling blind and deaf. In some cases they'll be all you have to get you through. Mostly, though, eye accessing cues will be a checkpoint on the route to high states of rapport.

You will be using eye accessing cues to assist you in strategy elicitation and playback to make sure you're using someone's correct neural network. You'll be using eye accessing cues in anchoring to really pack a walloping trigger for closings. You'll be using them as well in NLP power language to bring people into light trance states, making your suggestions very plausible. The fact is, eye accessing cues will be a mainstay of your power for as long as you choose to use NLP.

To facilitate the learning process, I'm going to give you a series of questions you can ask people so that you may watch eye accessing cues at work. In each category, you'll notice the questions are based on accessing a specific representational system. They are designed to get people to demonstrate their range of eye accessing cues, and have no significance except for demonstration purposes. You may synthesize and ask your own questions, as long as they bring people into the various representational areas you want to observe.

VISUAL REMEMBERED

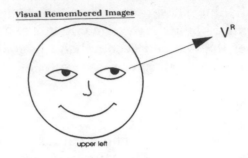

Visual Remembered Images

V^R

upper left

Q: Can you recall your first business office and what it looked like?

Q: Do you remember the lobby of the last hotel you stayed in?

Q: Can you recall exactly how many people were in the committee meeting last Tuesday?

Q: What color is your favorite business suit?

Q: Who was the last big client you entertained?

VISUAL CONSTRUCTED

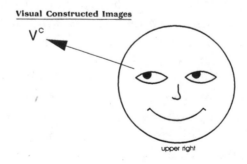

Visual Constructed Images

V^C

upper right

Q: What do you think you'd look like if you made a dozen closings today?

Q: What do you picture a million-dollar deal would look like?

Q: Can you ever see yourself relaxed with the boss?

Q: Can you picture yourself in a board meeting in your tennis shorts?

Q: Who can you see being the next big account you'll sell?

AUDITORY REMEMBERED

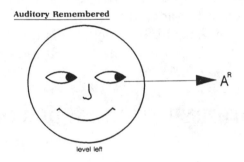

Auditory Remembered

level left

Q: What exactly did your boss say to you last week?

Q: What did your secretary tell you that was so interesting?

Q: Does the new VP of marketing sound like he knows what he's talking about?

Q: Who spoke to you about the new commission structure?

Q: Does your friend's secretary sound strange to you?

AUDITORY CONSTRUCTED

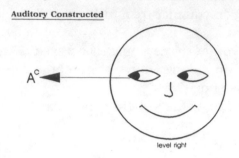

Auditory Constructed

level right

Q: What do you think they'll say about your new ideas?
Q: Can you imagine what they'll say when you tell them you've got the account?
Q: Have you heard what the boss is talking about?
Q: Someone said you wanted to tell me something.

AUDITORY INTERNAL DIALOGUE

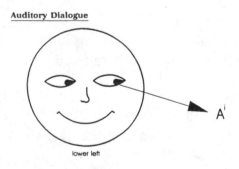

Auditory Dialogue

lower left

Q: Have you really listened to both sides of the story?
Q: What was it she told you that changed your mind?
Q: Do you remember exactly what he said?
Q: Can you recall what the boss said about that yester-day?

KINESTHETIC

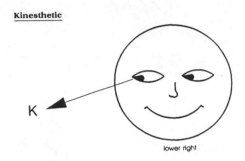

Kinesthetic

K

lower right

Q: How did it feel to get that promotion?

Q: You must have been proud of yourself when you closed that deal.

Q: Were you nervous in front of the executive committee?

Q: Were you satisfied with your last purchase?

In business, when we communicate with others, whether it's out in the field or at the office, our very communication stimulates other people's thoughts and provokes the feedback we receive. Since birth, we are almost exclusively trained to observe and respond to just the verbal part of communication. Eye accessing cues are simply another channel through which we can decode behavior, which helps us in returning communication. However, eye accessing cues are above the threshold of consciousness for most of us. That means that people can't control these cues because they are not in touch with the fact that their eye patterns have meaning. So eye accessing cues seldom, if ever, lie. The beauty in this is that we, as professional persuaders, have yet another tool we can use to manipulate the environment between us and another, so as to create circumstances that are beneficial.

8

POWER LANGUAGE

There is an amazing power hidden within the structure of language. This power derives its strength from the fact that language carries information coded within its flow, which speaks very loudly, openly, and clearly to the trained observer. Because NLP now offers us the ability to decode, rearrange, then recode this information, it empowers us with striking capabilities.

Our language—our everyday, garden-variety speaking language—is a wonderful display of our thoughts and intentions. For the most part, it operates well out of the scope of our conscious awareness, making it an ideal open door from which persuasion can enter and exit. This also explains why we are so very often misunderstood. We labor under the belief system that what we say is what we communicate. Nothing could be farther from the truth. The scientific fact is that what we say—the spoken portion of our communication—accounts for approximately 7 percent of our total communication package! If this surprises you, you're not alone. Most of us never receive any training in communication skills and have married the assumption that talk equals understanding. If you isolate this fact by itself and think about it for a minute, you'll get a glimpse of why our lives are spent continually trying to clean up the mess we make when we "communicate." And since we endeavor to clean up our communication garbage by further *dis*communication, we continue to get hoisted by our own petard. Now, if you segment the different parts of our lives where communication is totally vital to our survival, you'll get a larger frame of the enormity of the problem. And if you look at the most critical segment—our business relationships—you'll begin to see how amazing it is that we get as far as we do.

NOTHING ILLUSTRATES REPRESENTATIONAL THOUGHT BETTER THAN EVERYDAY LANGUAGE

Language is probably the best indicator of which representational system we're in at any moment. It certainly is the most obvious, and without doubt reveals the framework from which we're operating. It's a constant that travels with us wherever we go, especially in business. In our society the spoken language is nearly the most necessary component of communication at our disposal.

As already noted, we primarily generate thoughts in three distinct groups: visually, auditorily, and kinesthetically. Because language connects the gap between thought and representation, when we speak, we tend to language in the area of representation we are in. Specifically, if we're in the visual mode, we'll tend to talk in visual terms. That is to say, we'll phrase or couch our communication of that thought in the representational area from which it comes. For example:

Do you **see** my point of **view**?
Is that **clear** to you?
In customer relations, we must take the long **view**.
Can you **picture** what that will be like?
That's a horse of a different **color**.
Let's shift our **focus** and **zoom** in on that.
Are you **clear** about the new **perspective** we have of this?

Our internal representations of the world are so strong—indeed, they're our only connection to it—that we not only depend on them to represent experience, but base our communication of that experience on the representations themselves.

WE TALK IN THE SAME LANGUAGE AS WE THINK

When we do this, we use language that's laced with processing words indicative of our representational experience. Processing words, or *processors,* are the verbs, adverbs, and adjectives we unconsciously choose while talking, and they reveal which of the representational systems are highest in our consciousness. When one of the systems becomes strong enough to slip into our preconsciousness, our language reveals this immediately to the enlightened observer. Again, let me give you a few examples of someone who is either primarily auditory or in the auditory mode:

I **hear** what you're **saying**.
Let's fine-**tune** this presentation.

I think that brochure is too **loud**.
He strikes me as being a little **off-key**.
That **sounds** great.
I'm going to keep my **ear** to the ground for you.
It's **clear** that the two of them are in **harmony**.

This may at first sound incredibly simplistic to you. I know it did to me. It seems so logical, so obvious. In a very real sense it's quite literal. You see, our language *is* literal. When we talk about our experience, we speak in processors that indicate which representational system we're coming from.

Now let's put one and one together. If someone is talking visually—if he is using processors that are visual—it means one or both of two things. *It means that he is either in the visual mode at that moment or that he is a visual personality.* Either way, you have ascertained an incredible assist. And that's because of this:

> **PEOPLE IMMEDIATELY FEEL MORE COMFORTABLE, OPEN, AND IN RAPPORT WITH SOMEONE WHO'S *RESPONDING* TO THEM IN THE SAME REPRESENTATIONAL LANGUAGE AS THE ONE THEY'RE COMMUNICATING IN.**

When you feed back to someone information coded in the same representational language as they're talking in, it immediately opens the window of rapport. But more than that, it begins a process of trust and acceptance that can be ethically used within the context of selling.

You would be hard-pressed to communicate in a representational language different than the one you're thinking in. To do so, you'd have to have all your consciousness and awareness on not only *what* you're saying, but *how* you're representationally thinking about it. I don't know too many people who can do that.

Kinesthetics respond to processing words that code internal or external information in sensory-based language. For example:

> Let's try to get a **handle** on this.
> I think we can **firm up** the deal.
> I **strongly sense** that he's interested in the product.
> She is thinking about a **hands-on** system.
> Do you **feel** you're ready to close?
> I know in my **heart** you're right.
> **Deep down inside**, I have a **gut feeling** she's **terrific**.

When we return communication coded in precisely the same representational system as the one in which it was delivered, we immediately generate rapport.

CREATING RAPPORT, AND THE FURTHERING OF INFLUENCE THROUGH LANGUAGE MODELING

Talking in the same representational language as another will make selling almost effortless. It will open up new and exciting avenues for you to explore. Instead of struggling to gain the trust and confidence of a prospective customer, you'll be able to cut through the pea soup of indifference and indecision and move right to the heart of your sale. Instead of fighting for your boss's attention, you'll find her easier to talk with. Ideas will be considered and accepted in a way that may at first seem strange to you. You'll actually be able to be more ethical when you use NLP because it provides an extremely clean line of communication. You will become more credible. Your managers and colleagues will like you more. You will like them more. You see, it's a two-way street. When you model people's physical behavior, as we learned to do in mirroring, you really cause a wave of rapport to swell. When you continue on with language modeling, you break open heretofore rock-hard defenses. You become extremely powerful. You become a closer. A winner. Statistics go way up.

Like life, NLP's context is amazingly simple; on the other side of that realization is the fact, that, like life, NLP also deals with a very complex issue: change. Change, as far as I'm concerned, is the central thesis around which our lives are structured. Change is elusive yet obtainable; it is usually profound, yet is often simple in its structure; it's easily explained, but not so easily achieved. More than anything else, though, change gives us hope. Without change, or the power to change, our lives and our philosophy would be static. We'd never progress because there would be nothing to progress *to*. Therefore, having at least the power to change is quite important. Models offering the possibility of change are *important* models for us. And those that actually empower us to change or create change in others are enormously valuable. NLP is one of those relatively rare powerful models of change.

When we match the exact representational language of someone else, we're immediately causing rapport. Further, this process of rapport generation is being conducted on an unconscious basis. Now, if you code within that language of rapport the guts of what you're seeking to communicate—such as a closing or a sale or a presentation—that other individual is receiving information coded in such a way so as to be the most convincing, influential, and irresistible communication he can possibly receive. In other words, you're "customizing" your communication so that what you're saying "fits" the person to whom you're talking.

Let me give you an example from a dialogue between one of my associates and a prospective client he wants to consult with:

> CLIENT: It doesn't look as though what you're offering appears to be what we want. We had long discussions about this, and we can't see how your workshop would change things.

Now, what we've got here is a visual client who's pretty set against contracting my associate's services. My associate, however, wants the account because he's convinced he can turn the place around. The problem is, obviously, how to get the chance to try. Well, he could begin by matching the man's processor words. They seem pretty visual. However, there is much more going on here than just simple visual language. But for right now, let's see how simply matching processing language can start the ball rolling.

> ASSOCIATE: Yes sir, I can see that. It's clear that what you've focused on is different than what I'm offering. And if you take a look at your project from a different perspective, you'll begin to notice how much better and clearer my workshop will be. It will literally make that department shine.

I want you to understand that simply matching processors won't magically get you the job. *But it will generate rapport and start a process of change* within a situation that otherwise would remain unchangeable. Matching representational language is the door-opener. When you add mirroring to this process, you then get a geometric effect. When you begin to mirror this man's body movements, his breathing, his posture, the way he's standing, his accent (if any), and other mirrorable distinctions, you'll be adding fuel to the fire of language.

Let me illustrate how businesspeople very often *mismatch* their prospective customers. I overheard the following dialogue in the Bloomingdale's furniture department.

> PROSPECTIVE CUSTOMER: Could you tell me about your queen-sized convertible sofas? I'm curious to know if they're really comfortable. Whenever I notice one, I get the sense that they're hard and lumpy and would be terrible to relax or fall asleep on.

> SALESMAN: I've never heard any of my customers complain. In fact, I always hear how soundly people are able to sleep on them. Let me play a video for you demonstrating this particular mattress, and you'll be able to hear for yourself how terrific it is.

Clearly, this salesman had lost a sale. When I witnessed this, it was like watching someone pick up a few hundred dollar bills, tear them in half, then throw them out the window! That's how criminal the loss of this sale seemed to me.

Let's look again at what the customer asked:

> "Could you tell me about your queen-sized convertible sofas? I'm curious to know if they're really uncomfortable. Whenever I notice one, I get the sense that they're hard and lumpy and would be terrible to relax or fall asleep on."

Do you notice that this person is talking with kinesthetic processors? Very obvious ones. All the salesman needed to do was reply in the same representational processing words. For instance:

> SALESMAN: I can understand what you mean. I get that feeling as well when I first think about convertible sofas. And the truth is, as soon as I sit down on one for a while or sleep on one, I get reminded of my childhood, with all those terrific memories of sleeping over at my friends' or relatives' houses. Remember how warm and toasty you felt back then? It's been a long time since life was that peaceful. Interestingly enough, when I feel like I need some "home cookin'," I settle down on our convertible with a good book, and next thing I know, I'm feeling okay again. And you know, today's mattresses are real comfortable, too. That's why I love selling these beds.

Of course, I could have used any number of metaphors. But right now, that's not the point. We'll talk about metaphors and stories later on. For now, just be clear that using the same representational language while communicating ethically and with integrity simply secures the sale.

There's really only one rule that applies to using processors, and that's to make sure you're using the same representational field as the other person. If a person's model of the world is auditory and he's being communicated to using visual processing, the resulting dialogue will be out of sync, out of rapport—it won't fit well. However, when we match processors, system to system, we're coming aboard someone's lay of the land, his map of the territory. We're talking in a language he not only understands, but feels comfortable with. Hence, we bring him closer to liking and trusting us— and that brings us closer to our goal.

Once we've mastered the process of matching representational systems through language, our next step is to use the process of mirroring and pacing to deepen trust and rapport even further.

Pacing and Trust

Combining the process of mirroring with processor matching is very powerful. It is probably the fastest way to have people fall into a very deep rapport with you. But more than that, this particular combination will deeply arouse people's sense of trust in you.

It's at the beginning of pacing where the seeds of trust are sown. So stating a very truthful fact opens the door of influence. Always begin your pace by stating the obvious. For instance, if your prospective customer is hovering over a newly displayed computer, you might say:

> "I notice you're admiring our newest machine. Quite a difference between this one and our previous model."

Truth.

> "I notice you were comparing the features on this model and that other one."

Truth.

> "As you can see, the graphics on this one are much brighter and the colors are infinitely richer."

Truth.

Now, at this point in time, you've broken through the rapport barrier. How? Simply by stating the truth. You've paced the client into a belief system of trust. He's beginning to trust you because you're telling the truth. Unconsciously, you're also setting up what I call an *agreement frame.* You're stating undeniably truthful events that he simply cannot disagree with. By doing this, you've set in motion an agreement state. What you do next will be experienced through a perceptual filter of newly established trust.

Continue on with trust building by pacing the client's objections. At the first stall, or at the first utterance of disagreement, seize the opportunity by agreeing with the objection. Sound crazy? Not at all. You're simply continuing your mirroring of the client's behavior. It works very well. My favorite example of this is the way I personally turn around objections. As a psychologist, I've always repeated key phrases to clients when I wanted them to expand on a particular thought. However, this works even better with selling because it acts in the same way as aikido, in that it uses the very objection itself to build rapport.

To continue our illustration:

CUSTOMER: I had a computer that used the same operating system, and hated it. It never did what I wanted it to.

SALESPERSON: You believe your old computer didn't work the way you wanted it to; that you hated it.

The client *must* agree with you because you are agreeing with him! And the reason he must do so is because you're stating unequivocal truths. This immediately leads to deeper trust, higher rapport. Actually, at this point, the prospective client is already having a subconscious dialogue that is saying something like, "This guy's like me. He understands me." So the best place to be when dealing with an objection is on the prospect's side. Align yourself with him—it's where to be when you want rapport.

POWER LINGUISTICS FOR BUSINESS

Power Linkage

When you feel it's appropriate, you may increase the power of your pacing by using six specific words to link the present situation with where you want the client to go with you. These six words are:

> "and"
> "since"
> "while"
> "as"
> "before"
> "until"

These six words, when used in an NLP context, have the ability to cause a light trance state in those you're selling. They unconsciously link a moment of now to a moment of future. While doing this, they connect one thought process to another while picking up the pace. This is especially true for the word "and." "And" is the word that should replace the use of the word "but." When you use the word "but," you're virtually canceling out everything you've communicated in the preceding statement. When you substitute the word "and" you're *linking* the two statements, and hence, the two thoughts (which may very well be unrelated). This can have amazing results. To continue our example:

CUSTOMER: That's true. It just didn't fulfill my expectations about what a computer could do for my business.

SALESPERSON: I can understand that. Those kinds of experiences can be very frustrating, and you can recall how excited you just got about the thought of replacing it.

CUSTOMER: Yeah, It would be great to finally have something that really worked [nods head approvingly].

You'll notice the first two statements continue the pace by stating absolute truths. The third statement, linked by "and," picks up the pace and turns the objection into a benefit for both you and the client.

You should know that because of the logical level of thought that these deep structure contexts have, very often what you pace with (the truths) and what you connect them to (the persuasion) need not have any relationship whatsoever. The only rule you need to remember is to begin with an agreement frame, or an obvious truth, and connect them to your goal. For example:

> "I can see you're browsing, looking for a shirt
> that will make you look good, **and** these
> Armani button-downs pretty much fit the bill."

> "You're searching for a new bank to handle
> your increased business, and you want a re-
> sponsive organization. **As** you've probably no-
> ticed, you will feel very at home here **since** you
> can see how efficient we are."

> "No one really likes to buy insurance—including
> myself. **Since** it's something that is really a ne-
> cessity, **and** while we fill out the forms, you can
> tell me why you want to buy it now."

High-Level Modal Operators

When you feel it necessary to pick up the pace even higher, you may use HIGH-LEVEL MODAL OPERATORS. They put an even more profound spin on the amount of influence and persuasion you're seeking to induce. These words have in common the fact that they are cause-and-effect pacers. They include:

"must"
"have to"
"require"
"make"
"force"

Always preface these modal operators with undeniable and obvious truths. Remember, you want to align the prospective client in an agreement frame before taking him to a deeper level of rapport. These operators are an excellent source of further persuasion and can be used in conjunction with other NLP linguistic technology to make things happen.

Let's continue:

CUSTOMER: But even if it worked properly, I don't know. I remember looking at the user's guide and being very turned off by the way it was written.

SALESPERSON: Boy, have you got it right. I happen to have this particular computer's manual right here, and I don't know if I should let you see it because just looking at it will make you see how you really must have it.

Now, in this last little exchange, I was doing a few things. First, I agreed with the customer, building an agreement frame. Second, I used *"and"* to connect the truthful statement with the pacing statement. Next, I used two modal operators (make and must). Then finally, to top it off, I answered him visually—in his representational language. I own this guy!

Embedded Commands

I also did something else that you didn't know. I used an EMBEDDED COMMAND. An embedded command is a word or phrase that is tonally marked with your voice to produce a command that speaks to the unconscious. People don't hear these commands consciously, but they have a very strong impact. I've boldfaced the embedded command for you to see:

> SALESMAN: Boy have you got it right. I happen to have this particular computer's manual right here, and I don't know if I should let you see it because just looking at it will make you see how **you really must have it.**

Embedded commands are extremely easy to learn and powerfully effective to use. There are only two rules attached to them: You must tonally mark them, and you should preferably include them as part of a sentence.

I use embedded commands liberally because they turn a thirty-minute sell into a ten-minute closing. They're also very natural. Oftentimes you use them without knowing it. The key in using embedded commands to influence others is to make sure they are tonally marked. By that I mean in some way changing your voice. You may effect change with pitch or intonation or cadence or volume. It really doesn't matter, as long as you make some sort of change or mark when uttering the command.

Here are some examples:

You may probably **need the software** today.

Give it some thought; then, if **you want to buy**, we can arrange terms.

You probably don't want to **buy the computer**, and **now's a good time to.**

It's not necessary to **pay now**, as I know **you want to.**

Needless to say, there are many different ways you can insert embedded commands into your communication. You'll find them extremely effective in selling, bargaining, presenting, negotiating, hiring, and firing. They are especially effective when used with subordinates and superiors. You may use them to communicate thoughts to the boss that you ordinarily would feel inhibited from communicating. In mediation, they are strong allies in the bargaining process. And in sales, well, it's obvious to you by now how powerful they can be.

Agreement-Set Phrases

One of the notions that should be on your mind when you're out to create a deep rapport is that people will be highly influenced by you if they think you're telling the truth. So to get people into that perception, you need to constantly feed in to their belief systems. The easiest and most efficient way of doing this is to build rapport by stating obvious truths to form a train of agreement.

"It's Thursday, **isn't it**?"
"Shopping around for a computer can be a hassle, **right**?"
"Having a head cold is the worst, **don't you agree**?"
"**I've noticed** you've been looking at this computer for the last few minutes."

Agreement-Set Qualifiers

I want you to notice that I often use qualifiers at the end of agreement-set phrases. They really tighten up your agreement phrases and add a profound hypnotic spin to them. Qualifiers are phrases like:

"isn't it?"
"haven't you?"
"won't they?"
"didn't he?"

You can easily turn any mundane nonagreement-getting statement into an agreement-set question with the simple addition of these tail-end qualifiers. For example:

- Getting a new computer is good business.
⇓
Getting a new computer is good business, **isn't it**?

- I can see you're considering buying a new computer.
⇓
I can see you're considering buying a new computer, **aren't you**?

These newly formed questions are a hundredfold more effective than the statements they were built on. They reach out to the unconscious and scream, "This guy's reading my mind. He knows exactly what I want, and he's truthful."

High-Action Modifiers

You can really turn up the power on agreement-set questions by adding what I call "HIGH-ACTION" MODIFIERS. This is simply a word that forces the unconscious to recognize an opportunity it doesn't at first notice. Usually there are two words that fall into this category: "have" and "must." Following is an example of how to fire up the previously mentioned qualifiers such as "aren't they," or "isn't it."

To continue our drama, let's say that the subject of computer warranties comes up. The prospective customer lets you know that this is an important criteria for him or his company.

This is a terrific opportunity for you to add a "high-action" word to your presentation.

> CUSTOMER: Does this model have a good warranty?
>
> SALESPERSON: I know that a good warranty is very important to you. It should be. And many people in your position view warranties as something they **must** have in order to see their way clear to making a purchase, **don't they**?
>
> CUSTOMER: That happens to be true.
>
> SALESPERSON: That's why **most** people in your position look at additional warranty packages as something they **must** have.

If you look closely, you'll notice I'm doing a lot of different things. But all I want you to do now is to notice the use of the high-action motivators, which I've highlighted. They markedly increase the probability of total persuasion.

By now, you're aware of how combining different NLP techniques can geometrically increase your power. You've probably also noticed how I "layer" these technologies even as I teach them to you. For example, let's look again at the dialogue above:

> CUSTOMER: Does this model have a good warranty?
>
> SALESPERSON: I know that a good warranty is very important to you. It should be. <u>And</u> many people in your position VIEW warranties as *something they* **must** *have* in order to *see* their way CLEAR to *making a purchase* **DON'T THEY**?
>
> CUSTOMER: That happens to be true.
>
> SALESPERSON: That's why **most** people in your po-

sition LOOK at additional warranty packages <u>as</u> something *they* **must** *have.*

Besides adding high-action words, you'll notice that there are a few embedded commands sprinkled in. They are in italics.

Notice the modal operators, which get the customer's agreement and reinforce trust and rapport. They are in boldface.

The words in capitals are those that belong to this man's primary representational system. Remember, he's visual. So we build even more trust and rapport by matching his visual processing words.

"As" and "and" are power links used to connect one stream of thought—the truths of the buyer—to another stream of thought—the direction you want the sale to go. They are underlined. Also notice the qualifier to the agreement-set phrase in boldface caps.

Phonological Ambiguities

PHONOLOGICAL AMBIGUITIES are another powerful NLP technique. These are word phrases that have double meanings. But the way we use them in NLP makes them hypnotic in context. For example:

My friend Stuart is a car salesman for one of the General Motors lines. One of the biggest profit centers in his business comes from adding the electric windows option to an order. He told me that he could literally feed his family for a month on the commission from this one item alone. Obviously, he highly values the sale of this specific option. The challenge is that people interested in the particular models he sells don't usually have electric windows as a top priority. Economy is their highest criteria, and they're not terribly interested in luxury options.

One day Stuart and I had an animated discussion about this, and I told him to drop by my office, where I would show him exactly how to be in rapport with his customers while making sale after sale of the electric windows option. He hadn't the foggiest idea what I was talking about, but about a week later he came by—probably more out of curiosity than anything else. I explained to him how to embed a phonological ambiguity in his sales presentation to excite his customers about the idea of electric windows.

"A phonograph of ambi-WHO-i-ty?" he said, looking at me as if I had temporarily lapsed into Kling-on-ese.

"A phonological ambiguity." I smiled back. "It's just a very powerful form of subconscious suggestion."

"Ah, do you have to be a Nobel nominee to use it?"

"No, Stuart, just interested in selling electric windows."

"Oh. In that case, I'm all ears," he challenged as he settled back into his chair in the classic "Show me" position.

I explained that all he had to do was break up the phrase *electric windows* into smaller words or sounds and embed them into his regular sales pitch. In this case electric windows breaks up into:

ELEC / TRIC / WIN / DOWS

Now, all we do is insert the four parts into the normal dialogue of selling. Here's an example:

"If you **elect** to buy the car today, the **trick** would be to get all the options you want and a fast delivery. That would be a real **win. Those** are really the ingredients to a great deal."

What's happening here is that by shifting the meanings of words while embedding them in normal conversation, we place those we talk to in an *altered state*. This is possible because we ordinarily require that in natural language, only one meaning is communicated at a time. However, when we use words that have two different meanings in two different contexts—but which sound alike—we set up a highly suggestive rapport which can be easily used for deeply effective persuasion. But do we need to understand this to use power rapport effectively? Absolutely not! Just knowing how to form a phonological ambiguity is all that's required.

With rapport-rich power language you can play with many layers of NLP as you sell. For instance, I put a tonal marker on each key word, subtly lowering my voice when pronouncing it. In addition, when I begin to notice a behavioral change in a customer—maybe a tilt of the head or the beginnings of a smile—I'll anchor the customer to that state; in this particular case, possibly by slamming the car door while smiling. This way I have the benefits of the phonological ambiguity simply by firing off the anchor at any time. There are all kinds of powerful technologies for establishing rapport *around* businesspeople while actually *winning* their business.

To end my story, Stuart and another salesman are about to open their own dealership right in the heart of town. He recently dropped me a thank-you note, which I thought was wonderful because of the last line:

> ". . . next time you're in town, drop **by**. In **general**, you can find me in the showroom or in the garage fixing some hopelessly broken-down **motors** left for me by the service crew."

Touché, Stuart.

<<>>

The possibilities of combinations in the NLP game are almost limitless. Wherever there's a challenge, you can alter some form of power language or other technology to produce the desired effect.

I was once contacted by a legal firm about a problem involving the litigation of a tough and important patent infringement case. The firm was representing a large drug company whose former employee, a key molecular chemist, had leaked the patented formula of a very profitable brand-name drug to another company. They were suing the other company for unlawfully receiving stolen property and patent infringement. It was very complicated, but their biggest problem was one particular witness whose testimony could make or break the case. He was appearing for the defense and had literally memorized tens of pages of false testimony to make it sound as though what he was saying was the truth. But it wasn't. And no matter what the lawyers did, they couldn't budge this witness from his bogus story.

I agreed to join the litigation partnership as an expert consultant. I went to court and observed the witness being questioned. He was a pure visual representer. His language and eye accessing cues were strictly visual. And, I observed, he *had* memorized his testimony. During recess, I gave our lawyers a crash course in NLP and some specific instructions. I told them to keep this man out of his visual representational system and engrossed in any other system. I told them to speak in kinesthetic terms. And I told them to try to keep his eyes down and to his right when cross-examining him.

Over the weekend, the lawyers and I think-tanked around the clock on this strategy, and the next week we went to court and in one morning completely discredited this witness. As I instructed him, our attorney questioned the witness while standing in front of him at the testimony box. Whenever the witness spoke, our attorney would tap his pencil on the wooden divider running across the top of the witness stand, distracting the man's eyes down and to his right. He then found it next to impossible to remember the written dialogue because he was being cut off from his visual memory, where he stored pictures of the memorized script. This single strategy saved the drug company tens of millions of dollars. And all because of a little white magic that, while being used ethically, made a huge difference.

I want you to take a few moments right now and do some practice. I want you to create ten instances in which you could use at least one of the NLP power language techniques to effect change. Additionally, I want you to use them within the following frames or contexts:

- A manager influencing his department workers.
- A salesperson influencing a prospective client or customer.
- A middle management executive influencing her superiors.
- A boss speaking to the executive committee.

Next, I want you to *layer* two of the techniques together. It doesn't matter if it's representational language layered with embedded commands, or modal operators with agreement-set phrases, or phonological ambiguities with words that link one thought to another. Be daring. Combine anything you feel is appropriate. That's the trick with NLP. You must always be in the moment to decide what technology you're going to use to bring about the changes you want.

As a rule of thumb, it's important to remember that the more you layer power language, the deeper your level of rapport and the higher you'll be able to leverage your influence and persuasive abilities.

Now take five, and do some practice.

Transplanted Quotes

One of my favorite forms of power language is TRANS-PLANTED QUOTES. They are probably one of the easiest forms of persuasive subliminal communication. They're also, in spite of their ease of use, very powerful. I use them all the time, especially when I get lazy and just don't feel like doing anything more complex.

They work like this:

Let's say we're continuing our presentation with our friend the prospective computer customer—although if we've been using NLP, he should have been a done deal long ago. Let's cut directly to the chase by literally telling him to buy the computer—but framing it as though we're speaking to someone else.

> CUSTOMER: So far, it looks like you're right, I do need this system. But to tell you the truth, I'm still not totally convinced.
>
> SALESPERSON: I can respect that. It's oftentimes hard to make these kinds of decisions. Believe me, you're not the only one who agonizes over these things. Just yesterday, I had a customer from another company who was also teetering on the edge of making the same worthwhile purchase. I finally just told him, **"Buy the computer,"** and he did, and he's pretty happy.

Did you notice the transplanted quote? Can you think of how you might use transplanted quotes if you were, let's say, a stockbroker? Try these:

> "Just the other day, my friend told me to
> **'buy the stock,'** so I did."

> Or
> "After thinking about Polaroid, I said to myself,
> **'You must have the stock** for your portfolio.'"

Or

"Even so, all my friends told me, **'Don't miss this opportunity,'** so I figured to myself, **'This is a really good deal.'**"

Transplanted quotes are similar to embedded commands except they remain higher in the consciousness than do other suggestions. This is because you're actually using surface structure, such as the statement "Buy the computer," but reframing it to a third person, then embedding it in a deeper, more sensitive delivery system. I repeat this technique three or four times a minute while telling a story, and always as though I were directing it to a third party. I urge you to try it out. You'll be quite surprised at the ease and power of transplanted quotes.

Time Distortions or Time Scrambles

Another important tool in NLP power language is TIME DISTORTION. Time distortion statements make use of the mind's inability to effectively sort through statements which, in surface structure, don't make sense. But they pack a lot of power when wrapped around another statement, such as an embedded command. Here's an example:

To bring a client to a decision point about meeting you:

- "When is three o'clock tomorrow a good time for us to meet?"

To turn the corner in a sales presentation:

- "When is now a good time to buy that computer?"

To get a client to notice how much better things are after using your services:

- "Go to the next time in the future when in the past it used to be a problem to you, and notice what's different now."

Each of these time scrambles produces momentary confusion at a conscious level. But they are a very accurate and focused voice to the unconscious, where they implant the true message you're sending. That's the part of the mind we always want to talk to. Time scrambles are a bold way of getting there.

You'll notice also that I make liberal use of embedded commands and presuppositions in constructing these statements. A *presupposition is simply a statement that presupposes a fact.* In the time-scrambled statement

"Go to the next time in the future when in the past it used to be a problem to you, and notice what's different now."

the presupposition is

and notice what's different now.

We are presupposing that there is now, in fact, a difference. However, there may not be one. But your subject's mind will create one because it's being told to search for a difference. And when the mind is challenged in this way, it *always* finds an answer, because the mind always needs to be right. Presuppositions work because they make use of this reflexive, involuntary process.

State Shifting

When you reach a stall, it can be very frustrating—especially when you're very near to a close. This is true whether you're selling a product, a service, a point of view, yourself, or an idea. Oftentimes the prospective client or colleague may stall by way of implying that he hasn't the time to decide at the moment. I always use this as a cue to begin STATE SHIFTING. In STATE SHIFTING, we simply restate the stall but substitute a key word. My favorite use of this is when people say, "When I have a chance . . ."

- "When I have a chance, I'll look into it."
- "When I have a chance, I'll get back to you on that."
- "That's something I'd like to talk about with you, when I have a chance."

You can turn these stalls into movement by restating the stall with an action word. For example, the stall

"When I **have** a chance, I'll look into it."

can be restated positively and volleyed back to the subject by substituting the word "have" with "take," as follows:

"When you **take** the chance, you'll look into it?"

This shifts the client's action-imperative. He is unconsciously forced to consider taking quicker action. I may even go further with this by restating it as:

"When you **make** the chance, you'll look into it?"

This creates even swifter action by asking the subconscious not only to create the chance, but to take action on that creation. If you're even more daring, you can restate the stall with the most extreme of these action-shifts:

When you **make** the **opportunity**, you'll look into it?"

Notice that I've also inserted an embedded command here. And I've changed *two* of the client's words *instead of one.* This is pretty daring, but it works beautifully and will often make the difference between success and failure in your presentation.

<< >>

In the following chapters, we are really going to turn up the heat and learn the technologies of NLP business strategies, NLP business anchoring, and how to create layers of deep rapport. You'll discover exactly how people think and how to use this knowledge to influence them at their most intimate and basic levels.

Because the use of NeuroLinguistic Programming literally causes people to do what you want them to do, it's necessary to have a firm grasp of what we've learned so far. The following chapters will be somewhat dependent on the facility you have with what you've learned up to now. So this would be a good time to kick back, make yourself comfortable, and refamiliarize yourself with representational systems, eye accessing cues, and mirroring. Then full steam ahead.

9

GAINING POWER AND CONTROL WITH STRATEGIES

NLP, like a lot of other technological skills, requires a solid grasp of the basics before you can get out on the field and start playing effectively. Well, now you're ready. You've got a good grasp of what representational systems are and how to determine which one you're addressing; you understand the importance of mirroring and have found yourself consciously doing it with others; and yes, you're even getting more comfortable with eye accessing cues, finally being able to distinguish between your left and someone else's, and you've gotten through the previous chapter on power language and came out in one piece. Now then, it's a perfect time to begin our study of advanced NLP. Learning about strategies is the crux of this endeavor.

To begin with, let's get a basic understanding of what a strategy is.

You might say that a strategy is a game plan, or a set of actions that one takes in order to create a specific result. Each and every one of us has used the word *strategy* in that context. You might have heard it in sports, where strategies are everything. You've probably used the word in trying to communicate to another what you're going to accomplish in a certain regard. I know I have. I love tennis, and when you play tennis seriously, you've got to understand what strategies are all about. You must have a plan. If you don't, your opponent will steamroll you. It's not enough to just go out there and whack the ball as hard as you can. Lendl used to play like that. He'd step out on the court and belt the ball to Mars and make some incredible points—until he came up against McEnroe. Mac is a master strategist. Sure, he has plenty of power; his first serve was one of the best in the business. But it wasn't his power that made him number one for five straight years. It was his use of strategies. He was so adept at using strategy that even his serves had reasoning behind them. They were the most disguised serves in the sport. And that's how he would murder Lendl. He would feed him a game of tennis that Lendl just couldn't digest. So you might say that McEnroe's strategy with Lendl was to appear to have no strategy. By that I mean Mac would constantly change up his game so that Lendl, a player who craved consistency, had to deal with a tennis game consisting of no consistency whatsoever. I call that brilliant.

All of you are probably most familiar with business strategies. The company you work for has all sorts of strategies with which to market, advertise, promote, manufacture, design, install, sell, and enroll its product and/or services. Businesspeople know that using any number of specific selling strategies simply works better than just going out there alone and selling nakedly. Corporations spend hundreds of millions of dollars every year in the development of all sorts of strategies—so much so that the degree of overkill is just monumental. But it does prove one thing: Using strategies to accomplish a particular goal simply makes good sense. And the more specific the strategy, the better the result. Moreover, as you increase specificity, you geometrically expand the power of the particular strategy you're engaging.

Strategies have another key attribute associated with them. They enable whoever's *at* the controls to be *in* control. If you happen to be sitting at home watching television and get zapped by a commercial for Kellogg's Rice Krispies and that advertiser—by virtue of his ability to tap in to your cereal-buying strategy—pushes the right button, guess what? You're going to buy that cereal the next time you go food shopping. If you don't believe me, take a good look at what you buy the next time you go shopping—*for anything!* If you think you have a choice about it, think again. Ninety percent of what you take home—whether it's a box of cereal or a brand-spanking-new car—is a direct function of how well some huge corporation has run your particular buying strategy. In effect, intelligent advertisers, by dint of their mind control, determine what you buy even before you realize you need their product! Indeed, often the need itself is a result of a smoothly executed advertising campaign. That's just the way it is.

Advertisers have long realized the power of strategy elicitation and playback. They quietly found out that if they could find exactly what makes someone buy something, they could design their advertising campaign around this particular formula, sit back, and watch the dough roll in. Now, notice I didn't say anything about the design or quality of their product or what intrinsic good it may do. What I'm talking about here is strictly the *perception* they're able to give the consumer. Corporations have always relied heavily on perception; not on whether their product or service did the best, or even if it actually did what they claimed, but simply on how their product or service *seemed* to work. If it fulfilled success in that category, they were happy. And, basically, so were we. That's how well strategies worked for them. Until Japan woke up. But that's a whole other story.

The point is that people have wired into their brains an exact blueprint, or formula—or schematic or design, or arrangement—of exactly what it takes for them to reach the threshold of acceptance of any idea. In other words, for every behavior we have—and we have thousands of them—we have a corresponding formula of what we must go through—what mental steps we must personally take in terms of thought process—to achieve action on that behavior. It's like an on/ off switch. We don't take action on anything unless it fulfills the *exact* formula we have internalized in our brains for doing it. So if we see a chocolate ice-cream cone, we won't be able to eat it unless it completes our schematic, or *strategy*, for eating it.

A moment ago I mentioned that perception was the main criteria of useful strategies. It is. However, one must be sure to keep in mind that if all one does is sell perception, then one day—and it happens to all of us—the perception either won't be enough or the strategy generating that perception will fall bankrupt. In either case, the result is the same: failure to produce the result you want. Further, if your use of strategies had generated trust and rapport, you can scratch that particular relationship off your list for good. Nothing destroys power and rapport and trust quicker than the collapse of an empty strategy. Nothing.

Now that I've acquainted you with the notion of strategies, I want you to see that, like sportsmen and advertisers, we all have our personal business strategies.

A strategy, then, is a specific number of mental or psychological steps one needs to take in order to begin to fulfill a specific behavior. That behavior could literally be anything. It could be selling, buying, hiring, firing, servicing, installing, teaching, producing, writing, presenting, interviewing, organizing, planning, lecturing, communicating, and a thousand others that we use in business every day. The point is that, while each of us has his or her own strategy for doing something, there exists an equal and parallel formula for breaking the *code* to that particular strategy. Now, why would one want to break another's strategy code for the way he or she accomplishes a specific behavior—especially a behavior that is singularly that person's?

Strategies provide us with a set of psychological finger-prints across the neurology of a person's personality. If we're given a way to duplicate these fingerprints, and then a technique for activating them, it's akin to being supplied with the correct numbers to the lock on a safe. If you know the numbers, *and if you use them in the correct order,* the safe will pop open and the contents will be yours. People use these psychological combinations, or strategies, to perform all the behaviors in their entire constellation of personality. These behavioral repertoires pretty much stay the same for life, except in the case where one consciously chooses to alter a strategy by reframing it with a substitute strategy. But most people never get around to installing new behaviors, even when the behavioral strategy they presently use is self-destructive. Why else would people suffering from acute obesity still visit the pizza parlor and soda fountain? Why else do people continually run their relationships in the same disastrous and nonworking mode as they always have? And why else do people suffer at the hands of business opportunity when they could be prospering from the same set of conditions? The answer to these questions is, of course, that people are at the mercy of their own flawed strategies.

The mind, for our purposes, is a billion-megabyte hard-disk drive whose purpose is to hold, process, and spin out the many linear and multidimensional stacks of recorded representations we accumulate. One of the most wonderful things about this fact is that the mind loves familiarity. In fact, it will go out of its way to gravitate toward anything that is familiar. Another way of putting this is that the mind always seeks to be congruent. It wants to fit well with whatever incoming data it should meet up with.

> ## THE MIND IS A STACK OF REPRESENTATIONS. IT IS A MULTISENSORY LINEAR ARRANGEMENT OF TOTAL RECORDS OF SUCCESSIVE MOMENTS OF NOW.

To the mind, a strategy is a blueprint or schematic that is made up of representations. Some strategies have tens or even hundreds of representations. Others have as few as two. For our purposes, we will confine ourselves to three-step strategies because, in business, that's all we'll need to know to create positive change. So a strategy is the blueprint or formula for a particular behavior—and it contains three distinct representations.

We already know that we represent experience in one of three ways: visually, auditorially, or kinesthetically. So each representation may be either visual, auditory, or kinesthetic. It follows, then, that strategies are made up of pictures, sounds, and feelings representative of our experience. Let me give you an example by continuing our little drama taking place between the salesperson and the prospective computer customer from the last chapter:

SALESPERSON: Let me ask you, Mr. Prospect, is this your first experience buying a computer for the office, or have you had the opportunity of buying one previously?

CUSTOMER: Actually I bought our first system, a plain word processor, a while back. Great machine, but obviously limited in its applications. It didn't give us enough power. When you sat down at the keyboard you didn't get the feeling it could do the job fast enough. I kind of knew that when I first laid eyes on the thing, but I didn't know a whole lot about computers then, so I just said to myself, "There's only one way to learn," and I bought it. It served us okay.

If you take a good look at our continuing example, you'll probably notice some obvious points. You'll see that the prospect has certain criteria for buying computers. He likes power; and he likes many options. But it's really not enough to simply offer him back power and options. It's too gross. Too bulky. It *will* help you a bit. I mean, it *is* information. But unless this buyer is really one-dimensional, it wouldn't appear that you have enough data to easily sell him.

However, suppose we look further at this dialogue. Suppose we look beyond his stated needs and the content of what he said, and instead concentrate on what his subjective experience is telling us. Above and beyond his verbal communication, which only accounts for about 7 percent of what he's communicating, the client has provided us with a rich base of coded information. Somewhere hidden in his reply is the answer to the question of how to sell him. Can you find it? Look again:

CUSTOMER: Actually I bought our first system, a plain word processor, a while back. Great machine, but obviously limited in its applications. It didn't give us enough power. When you sat down at the keyboard you didn't get the feeling it could do the job fast enough. I kind of knew that when I first laid eyes on the thing, but I didn't know a whole lot about computers then, and I just said to myself, "There's only one way to learn," so I bought it. It served us okay.

If you discontinue attending to his *drama* or *content*, you'll notice that the customer is using key words to describe his sensory experience. In fact, he's using specific words that are perfectly parallel to how he's experiencing his perception. Moreover, if you look even closer you'll notice that he's using this descriptive information within the context of *how he buys computers.* You see, the salesperson has cleverly asked the client if he's ever bought a computer before. This forced the client to search out his experience in an effort to find an answer that corresponds to the request: specifically, *an experience in which he bought a computer.* Once the prospective client seizes that experience from his stack of representational memories, half the salesman's work is done.

In the client's answer below, I'm going to highlight his *representational responses:*

CUSTOMER: Actually I bought our first system, a plain word processor, a while back. Great machine, but obviously limited in its applications. It didn't give us enough **power**. When you sat down at the keyboard you didn't get the **feeling** it could do the job **fast enough**. I kind of knew that when I first **laid eyes on** the thing, but I didn't know a whole lot about computers then, and I just **said to myself**, "There's only one way to learn," so I bought it. It served us okay.

It should be obvious to you that the client has expressed his previous experience with language that is sensory rich. This almost always happens when you ask someone to recall specific experiences. If it doesn't, not to worry. In a little while we'll discuss exactly what to do about that.

Let's take a closer look at the specific representational words the customer used:

POWER
FEELING
FAST

LAID EYES ON
SAID TO MYSELF

Does anything seem familiar? Right! These words indicate that the client is expressing his memory with *representational* language. That is to say, he's experiencing a few different thoughts through his various representational systems. The words POWER, FEELING and FAST are kinesthetic words. They describe feelings. The phrase LAID EYES ON is visual in nature because it describes a visual experience. And finally, SAID TO MYSELF is auditory in nature because it illustrates an auditory experience. In all, we have three separate steps to this client's recall of buying a computer.

There is one final but critical component to this equation. And that's the order in which our prospective customer is using his representational thought. Order—or *syntax*, as it's called—is incredibly important. It is not enough to simply know someone's representations. You MUST have the syntax attached to the memory. Let me give you that again:

> **WHEN ELICITING SOMEONE'S STRATEGY,
> THE ORDER—WHAT WE CALL SYNTAX—OF
> THAT PERSON'S REPRESENTATIONS IS
> CRITICALLY IMPORTANT.**

Without syntax you might as well be shooting in the dark. It would be like having all the right notes to a wonderful song, but not knowing the order in which they are played. No song, right? How about knowing the words to a very moving speech, but not their order? Tell me, do you notice any difference in the following two phrases?

Ask not what your country can do for you, but what you
can do for your country.
Do country not for what your country but what you can
ask for your do can you.

Well, strategy elicitation and playback are just like this.
If you haven't the correct order, you haven't got the sale—
whether the sale is a customer, a coworker, a request for
promotion, or a presentation. If you can't string people's
thoughts together in a way that makes sense to *them*, you're
wasting your time. That's how important syntax is. It's the
difference that makes the difference.

When we know the different notes to a song and are then
able to string them together in the precise order in which
they were written, we've got a terrific chance of recreating
the song as the composer originally intended. If we then add
our own style to the treatment, we have a song reproduced
with our own interpretation of it.

Well, strategies are just like that. We elicit someone's
specific behavior for doing something (his song), we inter-
pret his notes and the order that they're played in (his syntax), we assemble our arrangement of it in the same way
(recoding), then we play it back to create something familiar
and irresistible to him (his strategy). When you do this correctly, you're offering the client a deal he can't refuse. You
see, you're offering back to him a mirror image of his critical
criteria for that specific strategy. If it's a prospective customer's buying strategy, you're making it irresistible for him
to buy what you're selling; if it's your boss's raise-giving or
promotion strategy, you're making it irresistible for her to
give you a raise or promotion; if it's her presentation strategy,
you're making it irresistible for her to love your presentation.
And so on, for any strategy. I'm sure that with imagination
you will immediately see the incredible usefulness of this
technology.

<< >>

Why does strategy elicitation and playback work?

The mind depends on its proprietary strategies for everything. From birth, as part of the developmental process, we develop our very own strategies for doing things. We say that's "our way" of behaving. Sometimes our strategies are modified by our parents, our friends, life, circumstances, and certainly experience. But by the time we're in our teens the vast majority of our behavioral strategies are burned in. That's it for life. From time to time we change them slightly, but in the main, they stay pretty much the way they've always been. That's why it's so hard for us to make major changes. Like in dieting, or in our tennis game, or in the way we relate, or how we sell, or the way we communicate. These behaviors are so locked in that oftentimes it's a losing battle trying to change them, even a little.

Because of this law of patterns, once we're able to uncover someone's strategy for something, we've found the correct steps to take in order to greatly influence him—within the context of that *specific* behavior. Let me demonstrate:

Last November, a Fortune 1,000 corporation contacted me about assisting them in refining their customer relations department. I agreed to do a preliminary study for them and found that they were losing a ton of cash each week by totally mishandling dissatisfied customers. It's not that they meant to be rude and ineffective, but they just didn't have the skills to handle a massively expanding market while at the same time maintaining the perception of concern for the customer. They were fine at handling day-to-day operations until any sort of complaint came along. Then things would fall apart: Their customer service representatives would become overwhelmed; effective communication would fly out the window; salespeople would intervene where they shouldn't; management would make unrealistic promises they couldn't keep. To make matters worse, they were a service business, counting on close contact with buyers for their survival. So to keep growing effectively, it was imperative that they begin to develop at least a basic rapport with customers. It didn't take me long to figure out what procedures to implement to change things around.

About a month later, I took my findings and solutions to the vice president in charge of customer relations for the company. Upon meeting him (let's call him Carter) I immediately saw what the cause of the problem was. Here was a man who was a living metaphor for the very department he headed. He was insensitive, rude and not very open to change. He wanted no part of a "rapport technologist" (that's what he called me) or what I might have to offer, since it was wholly antithetical to his very nature. In our first meeting, he explained to me right off the bat—and very bluntly—that:

> "The only time we ever had a satisfactory experience
> with an outside consultant was . . ."

And then, just as I settled back to listen to his story, I realized he was about to hand me his decision strategy. Carter was literally going to tell me *how* he hires consultants. Although I was taken off guard by sudden good fortune (it usually takes me a little more time to establish *that* kind of rapport), I recovered quickly and went into uptime. *Uptime* is my term for the state we're in when we really open ourselves to notice all of our incoming experience. Since his decision was very important to me, I paid close attention. He went on:

> ". . . when this guy from L.A. came to see us. He
> didn't waste much time, just looked around a lot. But

I could sense he knew what he was doing. He had an air of competence about him. Good thing, too, because I wanted to really watch him and see just what he was going to do. I mean, what did he know that I didn't? Well, anyway, he made some changes that, I must admit, were interesting. But mostly, he sat and talked with every manager and explained what he was doing. That impressed me. I even said to myself, 'This guy was a good choice.'

"But since that time, every consultant we've had was terrible. Didn't know what the hell they were doing. And it was so obvious. All you had to do was open your eyes and look and you knew in your gut that nothing they could tell you would make any difference."

It was just that simple. He literally handed all his representations to me in one fell swoop. And when that happens, they're automatically delivered in that person's precise syntax. So all I needed to do was play back the cont*ext* of his strategy with my cont*ent*. Let me show you exactly what I mean. Following, you'll notice I've highlighted all process words which indicate specific representational systems:

". . . when this guy from L.A. came to **see** us. He didn't waste much time, just **looked** around a lot. But I could **sense** he knew what he was doing. He had an **air of competence** about him. Good thing, too, because I wanted to really **watch** him and **see** just what he was going to do. I mean, what did he know that I didn't? Well, anyway, he made some changes that, I must admit, were interesting. But mostly, he sat and **talked** with every manager and **explained** what he was doing. That impressed me. I even **said to myself**, 'This guy was a good choice.'

"But since that time, every consultant we've had

was terrible. Didn't know what the hell they were doing. And it was so obvious. All you had to do was **open your eyes** and **look** and you **knew in your gut** that nothing they could **tell you** would have any meaning."

You'll notice that the processors move from one representational area to another. The words **see** and **looked** are obviously visual. **Sense** and **air of competence** are just as obviously kinesthetic. **Watch** and **see** are again visual. And **talked, explained**, and **said to myself** are starkly auditory. Can you see a pattern? Look again.

When you take the representational information that someone hands you and feed it back to them, it automatically creates rapport. Let me give you that again:

> **WHEN YOU TAKE THE REPRESENTATIONAL INFORMATION THAT SOMEONE HANDS YOU AND FEED IT BACK TO THEM, IT AUTOMATICALLY CREATES RAPPORT.**

If you look back at what Carter actually told me, you'll notice that his representations form a pattern, or strategy. First, there's a visual cluster of words. Then a kinesthetic cluster. That's followed by another set of visual words. And finally he completes the strategy with an auditory representation. Graphically represented, it looks something like this:

VISUAL   KINESTHETIC   VISUAL   AUDITORY
or
$$V \Rightarrow K \Rightarrow V \Rightarrow A$$

Now, this is my favorite part because there's a lot you can do with these magical representations. In fact, I'm going to demonstrate a few of the effective spins you can produce. But don't try to do all of these techniques the first few times out. It's enough—more than enough—to simply run someone's strategy back. It does the job terrifically. Later on you can add the fancy footwork and really have total control of any situation.

What I'm going to show you is an exact transcript of my response to Carter's discourse on consultants. Notice how I played back his decision strategy of $V \Rightarrow K \Rightarrow V \Rightarrow A$, using my own words. I'll underline each representation. Check it out:

"I can really understand your concern, Mr. Carter, seeing how you've come this far without satisfaction. Indeed, since you never hire outside consultants, it immediately occurred to me that you really sense these things should be handled internally. And looking at it from a different perspective might make it clearer. As the time to have higher profits is never better, I quickly say to myself, 'Michael, wasting time listening for the right person is just putting things off.' You may think you're not ready for a change, but chances are you are ready."

Do you see what's going on here? I'm feeding back Carter's exact representations for hiring consultants in the specific order in which he supplied it. I'm following the exact behavioral formula he uses when he makes a positive hiring decision. Not *my* formula, *his* formula. Look closely.

"seeing" = VISUAL = **V**
"sense" & *"internally"* = KINESTHETIC = **K**
"looking," *"perspective,"* & *"clearer"* = VISUAL = **V**
"say" & *"listening"* = AUDITORY = **A**

⇓

$$V \Rightarrow K \Rightarrow V \Rightarrow A$$

⇓

VISUAL	KINESTHETIC	VISUAL	AUDITORY
step 1	step 2	step 3	step 4

If I know the formula Carter uses for hiring consultants, doesn't it make sense for me to use it while offering him my services? Of course it does, because we all have our very own personal strategies for doing the things we want to do *our* way. These strategies make sense to us, not to others. That's why we find it so hard to influence people. We just aren't taught to reach others on *their* wavelength; we're programmed to communicate on *ours*. One of the biggest "a-ha's" you're going to have when you use NLP in this fashion is how suddenly and incredibly easy influencing others is.

All right, then. Let me tell you how things turned out with Mr. Carter. And while I'm doing that, I'll show you some of the techniques I used at the same time.

While noting his decision strategy (I was actually brazen enough to write it down in front of him), I began mirroring him by lightly tapping my pencil in time to his respirations, which I could see laboring against his vest. I began mirroring his other gestures. I then decided to run back his decision strategy, including within it some embedded commands, a phonological ambiguity, and maybe an anchor when he responded in a positive way. I waited for an appropriate moment when a response was called for, then presented him with his strategy as I've outlined above. I also layered the other NLP technologies, one on top of the other. When you do this, you're revving up your personal power literally by an order of magnitude. You become irresistible. There just isn't any defense. Take a look at the same response exactly as his unconscious mind understood it:

> "I can really understand your concern, Mr. Carter, see-ing how you've come this far without satisfaction. Indeed, since you never *hire* **outside consultants,** it immediately occurred to *me* that you really sense *these things should be handled* internally. And looking at it from a different perspective might make it clearer. *As the time to have* **higher** *profits* is never better, I quickly say to myself, '*Michael,* wasting time listening for the right person is just putting things off.' You may think you're not *ready for a change,* but chances are *you are ready.*"

Do you see how I've layered or nested one model on top of the other? The method I've used to install these models is called *tonal marking* and involves the use of vocal changes. Whenever I installed a new layer of NLP, I simply either lowered or raised my voice, changed my pitch or tone, or did whatever I thought natural at the moment. The important thing was that I always made some alteration in vocal quality when installing an NLP device. Notice the following:

1. I told him to "hire me" using one specific phonological ambiguity, two separate times. Those are the words in boldface italics.
2. I used embedded commands and suggestions about what to do. Those are the words that are italicized in plain face.
3. I used the words "and" and "as" to connect two thoughts for an agreement frame.

4. I did all this while playing back his decision strategy of $V \Rightarrow K \Rightarrow V \Rightarrow A$. These words are underlined. You'll notice that there's one visual word, then two kinesthetic words, three visual words, and finally two auditory words—and, most importantly, they're in the exact order of his decision strategy.

Then I showcased my actual plan for improving the customer relations division. While doing this, I always and continuously reiterated his strategy for hiring consultants, so there could be no reason for him to reject his own formula of behavior. Carter was selling Carter; I just happened to be there while all this was going on. In fact, I'm quite sure that even though Carter listened to the outline I had prepared, on a deeper level he had already decided favorably. Actually, it would have been nearly impossible for him *not* to have had a positive response because his unconscious was locked into rapport.

Throughout my presentation I installed the visual anchors of my proposal by pointing to my presentation folder every time Carter nodded approval, and by absentmindedly lighting his desk lighter each time he would smile. That way, when he referred to it over the next few days, he got a terrific sense of doing the right thing. Then, as I rose from my chair, I said, "Mr. Carter, I really think the answers to your problem are right in that folder. I'll be waiting for your decision."

Well, I waited longer than I thought I would for his company's letter of engagement, which was appropriate given the rapportless shape they were in. Actually, I got a phone call with the letter—not from Carter, but from his administrative assistant—asking me when I could start.

The day I began, Carter summoned me to his office. When I walked in, he told me how glad he was I could make it and how—after giving it some thought—*yes*, the answers *were* right there in the folder of my proposal. And I thought it was pretty interesting that he kept flicking his desk lighter as he smiled at me. Carter got his company in wonderful shape in spite of himself.

Obviously, the power of strategy technology is something to be reckoned with. But in order for you to be able to use it with ease and have it consistently work for you, it's important to remember the formula for both strategy elicitation *and* strategy playback. Let's look at each for a moment.

STRATEGY ELICITATION

In order to acquire someone's strategy, you must listen. Very often people will *tell you* what their strategy is as they talk with you. In fact, I've literally *asked* people to tell me their strategy. And very often have received it just this way. You see, people have no idea that you're listening to them on a representational level and that you're picking out the precise steps of their strategy. What's more, they really don't care! As far as most people are concerned, you can sit around all day long and take their strategies apart one by one, as long as you seem interested and willing to play.

Usually what does it for me is to get the first three steps of someone's particular strategy. And as I've said, 80 percent of the time I get it free, just by listening; or I simply ask them for it. However, when either of these two situations don't work, it's time to *elicit* their strategy by asking them specific questions.

I do this by asking them—within the appropriate conversational context—the very first thing they can recall about the specific experience I'm interested in. For example, when I want to know a particular manager's strategy for hiring a psychological consultant, I might ask:

"Was there ever a time when you hired an outside consultant and found the job he performed to be exceptional?"

When the manager locates that specific experience, I might ask him to tell me—in sensory language:

"What was the very first thing that made you aware that you were satisfied with his work? Was it something he showed you? Or something that he said? Or was it a feeling that you got about him?"

Whatever the manager's first reply is, that's the first representational step in his consultant-hiring strategy. Notice that I guided his thinking by phrasing my question with sensory-rich processors. Whichever way he responds, I might follow by asking him for the next step in his strategy:

"After he (showed you, told you, made you feel), what was the very next thing he did to make you aware of how competent he was? Was it something else he showed you? Or was it another point he made? Or did you get another sense that he was right on the money?"

And again, listen for his response. Whatever else it is, it will be his second strategy representational step. And so on, until I got three distinct steps. At this point I've succeeded in ascertaining a complete representational strategy.

<< >>

To acquire someone's strategy for a specific behavior, you must simply nudge him into *thinking* about that activity. So if you're preparing a presentation for your boss and you want to find out his criteria for successful presentations, get him aside and ask him if he's ever been really and totally impressed by someone else's presentation. I guarantee you that he'll tell you, in representational language, just the way he wants it presented to him, if you ask him the right way. If you have any trouble, just jog his memory and his representations a bit by asking him to be sensory specific.

For example:

I recently closed a multimillion-dollar deal for my friend Camey in approximately fifteen minutes. Literally. She had been trying for months to get a particular sponsor to advertise on her television insert shows. But the sponsor's vice president of advertising just didn't seem to get it.

I met this man at a wonderful outdoor party at Camey's house, which overlooks the Hudson Valley. About an hour into the festivities, Camey got me aside and pointed him out, whereupon the two of us made it our business to have me "accidently" bump into him. Following our little plan, it wasn't any trouble to mosey my way over to where he stood, right where you could see the valley itself. After I introduced myself and we shared some small talk about the magnificent view, I asked him about his business, getting a little more specific as we went along, trying not to seem too pushy. By the time he explained to me what he does, I was already in rapport with him through heavy-duty mirroring and matching. At that point I asked him what kind of media he traditionally used for advertising. He told me they had always used magazines. I asked him if, while advertising in magazines, he ever had an occasion in which a particular campaign was highly successful. I watched his eye accessing cues and listened to his processing words to acquire *his* strategy for successful advertising. He told me that about a year ago his company ran an ad that explained how his product could protect children (his eyes went lower right), while making the house bright and clean (his eyes went upper left and right). He went on to say that he personally thought it was a terrible ad, but that he couldn't argue with numbers.

So I asked again—now even more specifically—to recall any advertising they had done that he *personally* thought was terrific. He immediately perked up. With a tiny little smile on his face, he told me about the ad campaign that made him feel (kinesthetic; eyes lower right) how wonderful it was to be a child, and to remember the sense of warmth and security (again kinesthetic; lower right eye cues) it brought him. He went on to say that that particular campaign made it easy for him to remember his old neighborhood with the many weeping willows that competed for space with the open sky. He actually shifted states right in front of me. I immediately anchored him with a cough (we'll talk about anchoring in the next chapter)—then made note of his personal strategy for successful advertising. It was $K \Rightarrow K \Rightarrow V$.

Trying not to looked rushed, I excused myself and briskly trotted across the lawn, nearly knocking over a few of the other guests, and found Camey, who was engaged in barbecuing. I took her aside and told her what I'd done and literally begged her to try to close a deal NOW! Though she was totally disbelieving, she humored me and sauntered up to this fellow, who, as circumstances would have it, was still in a sort of semiblissful state. On the way over I told her to sell him using only the way her company would make this guy's product—or more importantly, him—*feel;* then at the end of the presentation, cap it off with how those feelings will make the product look.

"And, oh yeah, one more thing."

"What's that?"

"Cough a little."

"Why?"

"Just do it!"

I watched as my confused friend shuffled across the lawn and over to this guy, who was looking away and toward the river. It was some picture. There was Camey all decked out in a steak-sauce-stained chef's apron with a spatula in her hand; and here was Mr. Corporate America, in this semiconscious state, not knowing what was about to take place.

I watched from afar as they quite animatedly talked, my friend glancing over at me from time to time, me signaling with a gesture that mocked coughing. Riveted to the scene, ignoring a tray of delicious caviar that passed my way, I watched for some sign of progress. Lots of head nodding; lots of coughing. Nothing else. About ten minutes later, I saw them shake hands—the client now licking barbecue sauce off his palm—and each walk off in different directions. I caught up with Camey in the kitchen, where she was sitting down on her English cooking bench.

"Well, what happened?" I said.

"I don't know."

"What do you mean, you don't know?"

"I just don't know. One minute I'm looking after some medium-rare steaks, the next I'm closing this huge deal—in an apron!"

"You mean he went for it?" I said, grinning from ear to ear.

"That really doesn't describe it, Michael. It was more like he was *selling me!* But I don't understand what happened. All of us tried selling him not even a week ago. He couldn't have been less interested. Totally blasé about the whole thing. Now I walk right up to him, and he's open to me from the get-go. It was really bizarre. I did what you told me, going from feelings to images, back and forth. Then, feeling like a complete idiot, I pretended as though I had some hay fever and occasionally coughed."

"So it worked?"

"Did it work? We did the deal in the first three or four minutes. The rest of the time was spent talking about how this area reminded him of the neighborhood he grew up in, and how wonderful it felt to see the place again in his mind's eye. I have the strangest feeling I'm going to have a new weekend guest this summer. Michael, what the hell did you say to him?"

"We talked about our childhoods."

"Oh, right. And I suppose that's when it occurred to him how nice it would be to have my company do his advertising?"

"You mean you overheard?"

Strategy elicitation is about either actively listening for someone to tell you their criteria (as defined by representations) in specific order, or proactively asking them about a time when they had the kind of experience you're seeking to recreate. It's that simple. The key lies in representation and syntax. If you have those two, you're set.

STRATEGY PLAYBACK

When you play back someone's strategy, you're simply inserting *their* strategy into *your* story. Now, don't get hung up here in what a story consists of. That's the most common pitfall people make when playing with strategies. They think that there's either a particular *way* a story should be told, or a particular *kind* of story to tell. IT DOESN'T MATTER. So long as you stay within the general ball park of your subject area, it has practically no bearing on whether you talk about this or that.

Let me give you an example:

I was talking to the disbursements manager of a company I do a lot of consulting for. They traditionally pay very slowly, taking every day of the alloted contractual time before cutting a check. Being on the other side of the fence, I naturally like to be paid as soon as possible, and at this particular juncture in the calendar year, I didn't mind calling in all my receivables. I usually just hope for the best, but this year I got proactive about it and had some terrific results.

When I consult for a company, I never just do the training and leave. I always make myself available for follow-ups and additional consultations because I take pride in my work and I like to make sure they get a sense that they've received the best possible value. Part of my policy is dropping in now and then to see if I can be of any further help. Firms really appreciate this, and I get a kick out of seeing my stuff actually being put to work. So it wasn't unusual for me to run into this guy who's responsible for payables. Well, one day I took this opportunity to get paid a month ahead of schedule. And I did it just by running his strategy for paying quickly.

I ascertained just what representational criteria he uses to disburse funds by swinging around the conversation we were having to those times in his job when he feels compelled to pay quickly. The following is an abbreviated transcript of one part of that conversation:

ME: . . .and what do they usually do?

HIM: Oh, they're really thankful. You know, it's like they feel they've done an extra good job for the company.

ME: Interesting. But how do you decide *who* will be paid quicker?

HIM: I've never really thought about that. I've been doing it so long, I guess it's automatic by now.

ME: Can you recall the first time you ever did it? I mean, pay a bill ahead of the usual time.

HIM: Oh, sure. It was that guy who's famous for those time management courses. Sweet guy, actually, but didn't know a thing about time or management (laughs). He had a really terrific presentation, though. You always came away with the sense that you'd really learned something. I remembered how few times I actually felt that way after hiring an outside vendor.

ME: So that gut feeling was the sole determinant of you paying him faster?

HIM: Well, yeah, in a way. It's things like that which make consultants worthwhile. Even today, and I think it's gotta be some four years later, I can still see that time-line technique he taught us the first day. Use it still. In fact, whenever I look ahead at my day, I don't see the time, I see the appointment's face, and that helps me prepare that much better for meetings.

ME: So let me get this straight. This guy gives you a certain sense that his stuff will really work; you use it to actually look ahead and literally see each appointment; and then you pay him sooner than everyone else because that's what you consider good value. That's it?

HIM: What else counts, Michael?

I hope you can easily see what this man's strategy is for value, because it's precisely the strategy he uses for early payment. I didn't waste any time applying it—both at the time I was talking to him and two days later when I ran it again over the phone and fired off a few verbal anchors just to speed things along. I used the strategy of $K \Rightarrow V \Rightarrow K$ in everything I communicated to him—including my request for the balance of my fee.

After our little exchange above, I replied:

ME: It *is* important to feel good about the services you get from a consultant. And I think the opposite is also true. I think the consultant should feel good about the firm he's doing business with. It just makes for a better relationship. I mean, if you really, really enjoy working for your client, you're going to feel personally responsible for the work you do. And if in fact you do feel personally responsible, everybody—from the chairman, to senior management, to field director—will see it. It'll just be plain as day. And I've always agreed that seeing is believing. It's as clear as that day of yours where you see your appointment's face. It's as simple as that. Don't you agree?

HIM: Absolutely. That's exactly how I feel. I never thought someone else could see it quite that way.

ME: By the way, Peter, when *are* you going to **send me the balance of my fee**?

HIM: Consider it in the mail.

ME: Well, thanks. I like surprises.

Nothing to it. No big deal. Run the strategy, get the result. When I saw him a few days later, the guy was grinning from ear to ear. I had spoken the magic words, because they were *his* words, not mine. Fact is, I'm auditory, and my idea of a good job is having it sound the right way, not seeing it in focus. I couldn't care less about visual imagery or gut feelings *in this particular context*. But my friend does.

So, besides mirroring him, and using power language, and anchoring him to the super benevolent state he was in at that moment, I ran *his* formula for what it takes to write those checks. And as you've just seen, it worked. In fact, using strategy elicitation and playback works because you're persuading people and influencing people on their wavelength, on their lay of the land.

It simply makes good sense to give people pictures that make them feel happy.

10

THE UNLIMITED POWER OF ANCHORS

How do you spell relief?"

    "Winston tastes good like a . . ."

    "Aren't you hungry?"

"You deserve a break today."

What do these statements have in common? Well, a few things. They were all created by advertising companies; we could consider them slogans of one sort or another; and they do a good job of focusing us on their products. Tell me, then, when you read the third statement, do you feel your mouth water just a bit? When you read the fourth statement, can't you see in your mind's eye two very large golden arches? And in the first statement, somehow at that moment I don't believe you'd spell relief: r-e-l-i-e-f. The point is that these slogans aren't necessarily meant to deliver a literal message. Their purpose is to remind us of something that their creator has implied. In fact, when someone asks you "Aren't you hungry?" it is not the intent of the slogan to have you think, "Jeez, isn't that the Burger King motto?" No, that's not its purpose at all. Its true intent is to make you *desire* a Burger King product.

    That's what *anchors* are all about: to stimulate you into buying a particular product or service *without* your conscious mind understanding why. For once the conscious mind grabs on to the *meaning* of the message, the *power* of the message goes out the window. Think about it. Isn't it idiotic to spell relief: R-o-l-a-i-d-s? Yet, when the message jogs right past the conscious and straight into the unconscious, relief *is* spelled R-o-l-a-i-d-s. And make no mistake about it, you *will* reach for Rolaids. That's how powerful anchors are. In fact, anchors are so prevalent in our lives that we've selectively filtered out our perceptual experience of them.

Anchors.

I personally think of anchors as icing on the NLP cake. And that's how I tend to use them: to lock in a more basic behavioral change in someone else. But that's just my personal bias. I know people who use anchors in lieu of every other technology you've read in this book. And they're fabulously successful at using them.

This final chapter is not so much about creating change—although anchors do that unbelievably well—as it is about sealing it in, so that you have a lot of control over it. It's about being able to *re-create* change, or the *state* of change, at your pleasure. With the power of anchors, almost nothing will be beyond your reach. Yet for all their massive power, most of the time anchors are relatively easy to install and easy to reactivate. You must always keep in mind, however, that anchors are very much like computers in that whatever you put into them is exactly what you'll get out. If you install a strong anchor, you'll get a strong and useful response. But if you install a weak anchor, your work and your response will be for nothing. Like they say in the computer industry: "Garbage in, garbage out."

What *is* an anchor, anyway?

An anchor is a stimulus that provokes a response. But that would be way too simplistic a description. Anchors are stimuli; and they do elicit a response, but the way they are manipulated truly sets them apart from the stimulus-response model. Anchors are much more elegant in their applicability, and extremely subtle at their logical level of awareness. Also, anchors don't require the kind of repetition that the stimulus-response model does. You can install a potent anchor in one shot; and contrary to what a few experimental psychologists will tell you, their rate of extinction—that is, their ability to stay alive over time—is pretty good. I know people who are still walking around with anchors that were installed by various people in their lives twenty, thirty, and even forty years ago. Indeed, there's a good possibility that *you* have a few anchors directing at least some of your present-day behavior.

Anchors work by creating a response to a stimulus which had been installed at a previous time. Let me give you that again:

> ## ANCHORS WORK BY CREATING A RESPONSE TO A STIMULUS THAT HAD BEEN INSTALLED AT A PREVIOUS TIME.

An anchor is also a representation that fires off or triggers another such representation. And any part of a particular experience can be utilized as an anchor to access another part of that same experience.

It really isn't as mysterious as it sounds. In actuality, you've used anchors your whole life to affect and manipulate your environment. If your secretary knows not to bother you when you look or sound a certain way, that's because you've installed an anchor that produces that effect. I hope you didn't think it had something to do with her intuition, did you? If the boss is able to create feelings in you—whether they are feelings of empowerment or insecurity—that's because he's continually able to fire off that particular anchor, which you may have been walking around with for years. In fact, those feelings may have nothing do with any feelings or attitudes your boss has toward you. If you've been trying to sell a prospective client for the longest time and just haven't been able to pull it off—guess what? That client is triggering an anchor in your stack of representations that cuts you off from your natural ability to sell.

I once had a client who ran a huge medical center. He strongly believed in communicating how he felt about the staff directly to the staff, whether it was good or bad. If you screwed up and he found out about it, you could be sure you'd hear from him. The same was also true if you happened to perform exceptionally. He was one of those "one-minute manager" types who thought that, even after he completely bore down on you, before ending the meeting it was okay to grab you with a big bear hug and make like nothing happened. However, his staff never remembered his praisings, only his reprimands. He told me he didn't understand why this was so, assured me he read every possible book on effective management, and was following their rules to the letter. He was truly in the dark about why, no matter how much he would praise his staff, they only remembered how they felt after being reprimanded. I found out the key to this mystery literally in the first hour I spent at the hospital, accompanying him on departmental visits.

His problem was, in the main, that he was inadvertently installing a powerful negative anchor in his staff on each and every praising/reprimand. Since he always followed his scoldings with what he thought was a demonstration of support—a hug—he was kinesthetically anchoring his people *not* to the symbolism of the hug, but to the strong emotion of the reprimand. After that, each and every time someone on his staff was touched or hugged by him—including those times when he was praising them to the sky—they would walk away with feelings of humiliation. So he and his staff lost no matter which way it went. In fact, recently it had become even worse because everyone had generalized the anchor from a hug to the look on his face just before he'd hug them. You probably can identify with this in your personal life if you remember the times you came home to find your mate with a certain expression on her face (a visual anchor), or a tone in his voice (an auditory anchor), or a particular physical touch (a kinesthetic anchor), which produced a reaction in yourself that was contrary to how you felt just before walking in the door.

Now, the reason the hug was so tightly associated with the reprimand was that the reprimand elicited the stronger emotional response. Think about it. If someone first belittles you, then praises you, the initial sense of humiliation will overshadow any verbal recanting or praise that might follow. If you consider this in light of the fact that anchors depend on strong emotions to work well, you'll begin to understand what was going on. In fact, that's the first axiom of anchor installation:

ANCHORS DEPEND ON STRONG EMOTIONS TO WORK.

You would do well to remember this. When you install an anchor, you'll want to make sure your subject is as fully committed as possible to the emotion you want. The stronger the emotion at the moment of installation, the more powerful your anchor will be when it's fired off at a later time, and the longer it will remain intact.

When I saw what this man was doing each time he spoke with someone, I immediately explained to him what the problem was. The solution was simply to praise or reprimand in separate sessions. AND not to hug everyone. It took him a while to understand this, but eventually he got it and was able to contain himself. However, I had some seventy-five people on my hands who were totally and negatively programmed to expect grief just by seeing this guy. And it took quite a while to individually deprogram each one by collapsing his or her anchored responses. Eventually, though, things did straighten out. In fact, as I collapsed each staff member's negative anchor to the boss, I took that opportunity to install a truly positive anchor associated to the job. I would relax each employee, and have him recall a vividly exact and very positive experience he had while working there. If he couldn't recall one, I'd ask him to *imagine* one. That works just as well, by the way. When he had that experience firmly in his consciousness, I'd anchor him with either a visual, auditory, or kinesthetic anchor, depending on what his primary representational system was. Then I'd demonstrate how to fire off that anchor at any time to produce that same pleasurable state. And as a treat, I offered to install any resourceful anchor the employee wanted or could imagine, either in his professional or personal life. You wouldn't believe the requests I got.

There might be a few of you who are still wondering how anchors are beneficial, or in exactly which situations you'd use them. Let me cite a few examples:

- You can anchor your customers to feel extraordinarily receptive when you call on them for business.
- You can anchor your secretary so that he does particular tasks the way *you* want them to be done.

- You can anchor your boss to giving you a raise and/or a promotion.
- You can anchor the executive committee, or for that matter any committee, to readily accept your ideas.
- You can anchor *yourself* to be in a particularly resourceful state.

In fact, you can anchor just about anything you want as long as you fulfill anchoring's two criteria for installation:

I.
A FULLY ASSOCIATED EMOTIONAL STATE
AT THE MOMENT OF INSTALLATION.

II.
AN EFFECTIVE AND APPROPRIATE CHOICE
OF ANCHOR PLACEMENT.

I. A FULLY ASSOCIATED EMOTIONAL STATE

An anchor, for whatever reason you choose to use it, depends heavily on the exact emotional state your subject is in at the particular moment of installation. That means if you're going to use an anchor to increase your sales figures, you've got to be able to put your prospective customers in a potent frame of mind before you can anchor them. This is much easier than it sounds.

There are two ways to put someone in a particular and specific state of mind in preparation for anchoring.

The first is a **nonactive** method in which you simply wait for the subject to acquire that state on her own. This happens much more often than you're probably thinking at the moment. Recall some of the conversations you've had with clients over the past few days, paying attention to how they commmunicated their wishes to you. Undoubtedly you'll find that a lot of the time people become somewhat passionate about meeting their needs and wants. Now, when I talk about passion, remember that passion will look and sound differently in different people. Some people readily and obviously become elated, happy, restored, invigorated, aligned, etc., when thinking about what will please them, especially if they think there's a chance that they'll get it. Others will change with subtle responses. For instance, their posture and maybe their speech will change; they'll become more attentive; oftentimes facial color will change; their eye accessing cues will really start to become more pronounced. Whatever another's state change looks like, you must wait until he or she is at the highest point of their state before attempting installation. I call this being **fully associated.** When someone is fully associated, they completely or nearly completely step into their experience. If you think about it, you'll see that people get passionate much more than you think they do. You simply must be really present to notice it. Let me give you a typical scenario:

> You and your colleagues are in a meeting with the boss. He's actually considering using your ideas to market a new product. This is quite a big decision, as the product's fate *and* yours hang in the balance. At last, this is your chance to get that promotion. But wait! You're up against your old foe, a formidable colleague who's already been promoted twice—at

your expense!—*and* who always finds a way to dis-
credit your presentations. . . .

This is the time in everyone's career when they
either stay put in the day-to-day evolution of their
lives or shift gears and springboard into the arms of
opportunity.

. . . You sit upright in your seat as you speak up
to gain your boss's attention. All eyes are on you.
But, as usual, your competition interjects with a long
line of thought. You're in jeopardy. Suddenly he
stumbles over a simple fact that he just can't remember. It happens to all of us. It's right there on the tip
of his tongue, but he can't get to it.

You remember anchoring.

Thank God.

As your colleague searches for that word or
thought—in those six or seven seconds—you cough.
Maybe twice. Of course, no one pays any attention
to it. That is, no one except your colleague's subconscious. And you. Because you know what you've
just done. You've anchored this man to his forgetting
strategy! A strategy that's so innately powerful, all of
us have a basic fear of it. Now you wait. But not for
long. You give your presentation and it's good. No
objections. Your boss is smiling, and you feel as
though you're light as a feather. But then, once
again, your colleague interrupts:

"But wait. What about . . ." and starts to leverage
in the one variable you left out.

No problem. Why? Because as he begins to pon-
tificate, you simply cough. Maybe twice. Unbe-
knownst to anyone in the room, you've fired off his
forgetting anchor and he's suddenly having a problem recalling relevant information. He puts a hand
up and nervously quips:

"Ah, one second . . . I, ah . . . it's on the tip of
. . . [cough, cough] . . . this is amazing . . . if you'll
just give me . . ."

Meanwhile, the boss puts his hand out to you
(while you anchor the satisfaction he's experiencing
by touching his elbow with your other hand) and
smiles:

"I think we've heard enough. Let's go with *your*
winning idea."

You modestly smile and thank him for his time.
Grabbing your attaché, you swivel and turn toward
the door, making a graceful exit. But as you leave,
you casually give one last cough as your colleague
unsuccessfully struggles to regain his composure.

Do you see where the fully associated state is? The process of forgetting an important piece of information during
a significant presentation can be humiliating and quite upset-
ting. By sporadically coughing, you would link up, in your
subject, the intense feeling of humiliation with the sound of
the cough. In addition, in this particular case, you'd also be
anchoring the entire strategy of a momentary memory lapse.
So, indeed, this would be a powerful anchor. Whenever we
layer or stack one NLP technology on top of another, we'll
invariably produce a result that is four times as powerful in
its synergy. So the combination of the simplest of techniques
oftentimes yields the biggest rewards.

The second way to get people into state is by **proactively**
engaging them.

When you proactively engage people, you're gently nudg-
ing them into the kind of state you desire. You accomplish
this by asking people to recall specific times in their past
when they felt the way you want them to feel now—so that
you may use this resource state as an anchor for what you

want to accomplish in the present. In other words, you're asking people to step into the experience you want *now* by getting them to remember what it was like *then*.

One of the best properties of anchors is their quality of state reproduction without content recollection. In plain language, this means that when you install an anchor correctly, then fire it off at a later time, the subject will have all the raw feelings associated with that past state, but with none of the actual thought content. Let me give you that again:

> **WHEN AN ANCHOR IS ACTIVATED, THE SUBJECT WILL HAVE ALL THE RAW FEELINGS ASSOCIATED WITH THE PREVIOUS RESOURCE STATE, BUT WITH NONE OF THE ACTUAL THOUGHT CONTENT.**

I'm sure you can appreciate the implications of such an occurrence. This means that if you were to associate someone to a state of, let's say, acceptance, then fire off that particular anchor while selling her your product or service, the result will be someone who is experiencing a vivid sense of acceptance and openness without recalling or questioning what it is that's creating that state. Instead of the content recollection, her experience will be of you, and of what it is that you're doing or saying at that moment. She will be seeing you through a perceptual filter of whatever emotional state you've anchored her to. Are you with me?

What you must always endeavor to do, especially in proactive anchoring, is to get your subject as fully associated to the emotion as you possibly can. The more intensely he is in that emotional state, the better your anchor will be. By better, what I mean is how deeply someone will fall back to that state when he is reactivated at a later time. So if you're seeking a raise and you're talking with your boss about it, make sure you've sufficiently anchored him ahead of time to some really intense feelings. These feelings don't have to be content-specific. That is, you needn't bother to anchor your boss to a state of happiness *necessarily* associated with giving someone a raise. That kind of specificity is only required for running someone's strategy. With anchoring, you need only be concerned with context. In other words, in seeking a raise, for example, it is totally sufficient for you simply to get your boss associated to *any kind* of pleasurable state. Remember, anchoring doesn't depend on having people recall *what* made them feel good—just on *feeling good itself.* Do you follow?

Let me give you an example of a nonactive visual anchor by sharing with you how I secured the largest contract I ever had.

After what was probably the biggest search this corporation ever undertook for an outside consultant, it came down to three of us. I was thrilled about this because I had not been in the field very long and this contract meant a lot to me. The man and the woman with whom I shared the list were seasoned professionals who had been in the field some fifteen years. They were polished, sophisticated, and they knew their work. On the other hand, here I was, in a field that this particular company knew relatively little about, with this new approach to influence, and asking, as I found out, considerably more money than my competition.

When the day of the final presentations came, I found myself in a huge and intimidating conference room. After all, this was a major FORTUNE 500 company, in New York City, in the heart of the banking industry. The two other finalists and myself were to sum up our proposals for the organization and were to deliver them that day before a dozen officers of the corporation. Talk about being nervous!

The head of this enormous conference table was obviously where the chairman was seated because placed there was a chair that any monarch would have found comfortable. It was totally imposing. And so was the man who sat in it. Though fair, he was gruff and came right to the point, never veering from what he wanted to know. When he spoke, each and every head turned with such alacrity that you could hear the rub of neck to collar.

Well, my two opponents gave an hour presentation each, answered questions with finesse, and just generally faired very well. They were quizzed by everyone, but when the chairman spoke—in fact, when he did anything—whatever else was happening in the room at that moment was deferred to him. Even when a vice president was arguing a pretty salient point, if the chairman intervened with his perceptions . . . well, that's the way that particular point was settled. Clearly, this was an enormously powerful man who was a commanding decision maker. That point wasn't lost on me. I knew that no matter what else I did, if I could get this man on my side, I had it made in the shade. Trouble was, halfway through my presentation he was called away on some urgent business and announced that the decision would be made by a general consensus, then left the forum open for discussion. You want to know what fear is? Suddenly I was alone up there with twenty-six eyes looking at me. No one blinked.

At that point, they asked the other two presenters to leave. When they did, the most senior vice president turned to me and asked me to tell them why they should spend x number of dollars *more* on me. I knew that if I could do it here, they'd meet my price and I'd be home free. But what to do?

And then it occurred to me that I was totally equipped to handle this. After all, *I* was the expert in persuasion and influence, wasn't I? In a way, I think in retrospect that that's precisely what they had been thinking: "If he's so good, let him convince us."

At that very moment, I saw a terrific possibility.

I couldn't have ignored the fact that the seat of power in this room was at the head of the table in the form of the chairman. But he was gone now. The singular decision maker was absent and the determination was left to the dozen executives still sitting around the huge table. I knew I couldn't depend on playing to one or even four of them; I had to sell them as a team. I also knew that the way to do this was to give myself as much authority as possible. And then I recalled what politicians do when they really go for the gusto. They always have an American flag near them. They use the power and authority of the visual anchor of the flag to link themselves to credibility and integrity. Well, there wasn't a flag in the room, and the chairman had left, but his represen-tation—the one other article in the room that was linked to his power—was the huge leather chair he sat in. Of all the chairs at that table, his was the most formidable. What a fabulous anchor!

So as I was summing up my presentation, I began casu-ally walking around the room, always stopping right behind the chairman's chair to make an important point—like why my fee was higher than the other two candidates'. And each time I encountered resistance, I paused, went to the head of the table, leaned over the top of the vacant chair, and con-tinued. You had to see the physical changes in those people! Whenever I was at the chair, resistance was practically nil. Naturally, I was mirroring them and using the same kinds of power language we talked about in Chapter 8. But what did the trick was anchoring.

Finally, in the very last minute of the meeting, I walked around to the chair again and *sat down in it.* I looked out over the committee and told them that if they really wanted to see a tangible improvement in their sales, they had to hire me to design their advertising. In fact, I barraged them with about seven or eight embedded commands while using the visual anchor of the chair to literally force the choice.

After that, the other two presenters just didn't have a chance, and, quite naturally, I landed the consultation.

Anchor Installation

Installing an anchor is the most critical step in producing effective anchors. If you're successful at bringing someone into state, whether proactively or nonactively, but you don't install your anchor successfully, your mission will fail. Always make sure that your anchor is well placed, available for your use, somewhat unique, and intensely installed.

There are three kinds of anchors, and they correspond to the three major representational systems: visual, auditory, and kinesthetic.

Visual anchors are the kind that are obviously visual. The chair from the example I just gave is a visual anchor. The expression on someone's face is a visual anchor. A picture, color, movement, action—these are all visual anchors.

Auditory anchors appeal to one's hearing. The cough from two of our recent examples is a wonderful auditory anchor because it's invisible. Any kind of noise can be an anchor if it's paired at the height of a specific emotional action. I love auditory anchors probably because I'm auditory. I just tend to think they work rather well.

Kinesthetic anchors are linked to feeling states, and research demonstrates that these are the longest lasting of all anchors. Especially effective are external kinesthetic anchors that use touch. If you're a manager and you want to get the most from your team members, use kinesthetic anchors. Find a unique but appropriate place to touch someone and keep installing the anchor whenever possible. After a while, just touching that spot will elicit the feeling you want in your subordinate.

II. ANCHOR PLACEMENT

The *placement* of an anchor is all-important. If you install an anchor as a handshake, for instance, it won't last very long because people will be triggering it all the time. The same for a visual anchor such as a smile. Ditto for auditory anchors which are composed of everyday sounds. The uniqueness of an anchor paired with a really intense state of emotion as it's placed, will put you in control of situations that you wouldn't have ever thought possible. One of the anchors that I used for a very long time, because it was so effective and incredibly easy to install, was laughter paired with a squeeze of the elbow. Laughter puts everyone in a great state of mind, and because it's an intense feeling, people associate to it rapidly. Squeezing behind the elbow is a pretty good placement because the backs of elbows don't get squeezed very much in the course of daily life. Whenever I start a lengthy consult, I anchor *everyone* to their laughter. This way, when I start the sometimes painful process of change, I have the availability of great feelings at my disposal. I remember one guy, must have been six-three, 235 pounds, tough-looking. He didn't like the idea of doing things differently, and his was one of the few positions that needed change the most. Well, because of the anchor I installed the first day I was in his department, he literally smiled all through the process, even as they carried his desk all the way down the hall to a smaller office. "It's for the best," he said offhandedly to me. "I'll get more work done over there."

Generally speaking, I like to get as much repetition in as I can when placing an anchor. This isn't always possible, but if you find it open to you, go for it, and take every opportunity you have to repeat any anchor you've installed. This burns the resulting response right into the nervous system. The more repetition you drill in, the more effective the anchor, and the more spectacular the results.

Cross-Representational Anchoring

When you need to install an anchor in someone who is *clearly* visual, auditory, or kinesthetic, the best and most effective way to do this is through that person's *secondary* representational system. That means that if someone is, let's say, very obviously auditory, you'll want to anchor her through some other representational system than her primary one. In *cross-representational anchoring* we anchor others to their **non-dominant** representational system.

For instance, when someone attempts to anchor me auditorily, since sound for me is way up there in my consciousness and awareness, there remains the possibility of my discovering the anchor. So it wouldn't make sense to anchor me that way. But I pay the least attention to my visual experience, so visual anchors work well with me. Likewise, you wouldn't want to anchor someone who's extremely kinesthetic to another feeling state; so it would be wise to anchor him visually or auditorily. Using cross-representational anchors just makes anchoring even more effective because it makes your anchors that much more covert.

Layering or Stacking Anchors

Another way to really pack a wallop with your anchors is to layer or stack them. When you stack anchors, you're anchoring someone in more than one representational system at a time. This gives your anchors even further accessibility and allows you that much more spin and control in their execution. When stacking, it's important to install all anchors at the same time.

A friend of mine, who was in the same Ph.D. program as me, and who was also an expert trainer in NLP, anchored his oral defense committee to their feelings of recent vacations. At the beginning of his presentation, before everyone took their seats, he went around to each of the five committee members individually and fully associated them to the wonderful pleasure they just had on their month-long vacations.

He anchored them in all three representational areas. After getting them to recall the exact pleasures of their vacation, simply by being extremely interested and animated as he spoke with them, he shook each one's hand, grabbed his or her arm enthusiastically, smiled, and said YYYEEEE- EESS! He did this three or four times within an appropriate conversational context to each of them before the session began, deeply installing strong pleasurable emotions in everyone. At the break, he went over to each and found a way to do the same thing when talking about something else. And again, at the session's end, he repeated the entire procedure. The next day he phoned each member of the committee to see if he could answer any questions that might have come up, and after making sure they had his paperwork in front of them, took the first opportunity to respond in the positive with YYYEEEEEESS!—thereby reactivating not only one anchor, but the three of them. Needless to say, although he was a month late in his research design, he didn't have a problem with his dissertation.

For as long as most of us can remember, certainly since the beginning of the industrial revolution, people have continually searched for a better way to accomplish things. And from time to time, truly remarkable discoveries have been made. In manufacturing, it probably was the invention of the assembly line. In voice communications, nobody would deny it was the telephone. In computers, undoubtedly it was the chip.

It's my personal opinion that NeuroLinguistic Programming has, and will continue to have, the same kind of impact on human interaction that these other important discoveries have had in their respective fields.

NLP has played a major role in my life in that it has enabled me to dissolve the barriers between myself and the communication of myself. That's an important distinction, in my opinion. So much of what we try to get across in our interaction with people gets lost in the *vehicle* of that interaction. Our inner dialogues, our perspectives, our perceptual filters—all of these contribute to the mixture that we call "communicating." So much so that very often our intent is lost to the medium in which we communicate. NLP is a model of behavioral methodology that allows us to communicate cleaner and with much more clarity than has ever been available to us before.

There will always be those detractors who point accusingly at NLP and attempt to show how covert and manipulative it is. Well, maybe that's so. Maybe NLP is a lot like other technologies that depend on their operators to ensure their proper, appropriate, and ethical execution.

But consider this: Most of what we do, most of our behavior, in toto, is manipulative in that it always seeks, by definition, to have others see our points of view. And what a celebration that it does. For if it didn't, if we weren't able to get others outside themselves to listen, to see, and to experience behaviors and thoughts different than their own, we would cease to progress. We would slip away into the blue void of history, forever known as the human society for which creative exchange just wasn't feasible. Of course, this should never be allowed to happen.

What I want you to do is take the information you've gotten from this book and go out there into the marketplace and weave it into your natural ability to cause change. NLP works best when it becomes part of the fabric of who you are. It is not meant to be *the* singular tool of your presentation, but a very strong ally in creating success. When you implement it this way, you'll discover that it will empower you with a persuasive ability you've just never had before.

Use NLP as you would a new suit of ability. Reach into your closet of resources and try on NLP to see how it fits. At the beginning you may feel a little awkward wearing it, just like you would wearing a new suit of clothes. And like a fine garment, it may take some time before you're totally comfortable with it. But as time passes, and with each wearing, your new resource will become more powerful, elegant, and effective.

Remember that NLP is beyond the conscious awareness of those you communicate with. It will affect them on a much deeper level than any content you might express. So when using it, respect its power and the integrity of those you're influencing. The most significant thing you can do while using NLP is to make sure that in the process of influencing people you give them value. In fact, try to give two or three times the value you expect back. This way the change you create is lasting. Long after anchors and strategy playback have become a part of your ongoing relationships, the value you give will cement the opportunity that NeuroLinguistic Programming initially created.

Yes, combining this philosophy of value with the technology you now own, you will indeed become very powerful.

—AND BEFORE YOU LEAVE THE MARKET PLACE,
SEE THAT NO ONE HAS GONE HIS WAY WITH EMPTY HANDS.
FOR THE MASTER SPIRIT OF THE EARTH SHALL
NOT SLEEP PEACEFULLY UPON THE WIND TILL THE NEEDS
OF THE LEAST OF YOU ARE SATISFIED.

—KAHLIL GIBRAN, *THE PROPHET*

Index

MANY CORPORATIONS, BECAUSE OF THEIR DESIRE TO CREATE HIGHER SALES FIGURES AND INCREASED PRODUCTIVITY, AS WELL AS SMOOTHER AND MORE EFFICIENT COMMUNICATIONS, HAVE INQUIRED ABOUT TRAINING IN NEUROLINGUISTIC PROGRAMMING.

DR. MICHAEL BROOKS, AN INDUSTRIAL PSYCHOLOGIST, IS AN *NLP* TRAINER AND CORPORATE CONSULTANT WHO DELIVERS IN-HOUSE TRAINING SEMINARS, AND IS A NOTED PUBLIC SPEAKER.

IF YOU ARE INTERESTED IN HAVING THE BENEFITS OF *NLP* WORK FOR YOU OR YOUR COMPANY, WHETHER IN THE FORM OF LECTURES, CUSTOM DESIGNED PROGRAMS, OR TRAINING SEMINARS, PLEASE FEEL FREE TO CONTACT DR. BROOKS AT THE FOLLOWING ADDRESS AND TELEPHONE NUMBER.